JN329028

Funny Laws in the World

「世界おもしろ比較文化」

ー法律から学ぶ文化事情ー

Takayuki Ishii
Masahiko Iwata
Munekatsu Kajiyama
Joe Ciunci

NAN'UN-DO

Funny Laws in the World

Takayuki Ishii
Masahiko Iwata
Munekatsu Kajiyama
Joe Ciunci

Download Audio
音声ファイル
無料 DL
のご案内

このテキストの音声を無料で視聴（ストリーミング）・ダウンロードできます。自習用音声としてご活用ください。
以下のサイトにアクセスしてテキスト番号で検索してください。

https://nanun-do.com　テキスト番号［ **511678** ］

※ 無線 LAN（WiFi）に接続してのご利用を推奨いたします。

※ 音声ダウンロードは Zip ファイルでの提供になります。
お使いの機器によっては別途ソフトウェア（アプリケーション）の導入が必要となります。

※ Funny Laws in the World 音声ダウンロードページは以下の QR コードからもご利用になれます。

はじめに

2015年現在、世界には日本が認めている194ヵ国と日本を入れて195ヵ国があります。また、世界には主としてこれらの国に住む多数派の民族200程度と、3000ぐらいの少数民族が存在すると考えられています。世界の言語数となれば、方言か言語かが不分明で、微妙なケースがあると思われますが、約8000の言語が存在するという考え方があります。このように多様性に満ちた世界であるからこそ、文化が異なり、考え方も異なるのだと思われます。

本書では、法律の分野に焦点を絞り、世界の異なる国には、異なるユニークな法律が存在すること、そしてその法律は文化や考え方とどう関わっているのかなどを掘り下げつつ、英語をトータルな視座で学ぶことを目的としています。

もちろん、本書は、単語や文法の基礎的学習に基づく、英語4技能の能力向上を目指した英語総合教材ですが、現在、大学英語教育に不可欠な要素となっているTOEICテスト対策としても利用できるよう編まれています。

例えば、リーディング・パッセージの後の設問設定において、4択にしているものが多いのはTOEICテストのPart 5を意識しているからです。

本書は、企画案作成とテーマ設定、コラムおよびVocabularyを岩田が、各章最初のReading PassageをJoe Ciunciが、Comprehension、GrammarおよびCompositionを梶山が、さらに全体の監修を石井が担当しました。

なお、全体の編集内容と、設問のユニークな設定、その他有益なアドバイスを編集部の丸小雅臣氏にいただかなければ、本書は世に出ませんでした。丸小氏に心から感謝の言葉を述べたいと思います。

本書を通じて、英語の総合能力を向上させ、法律に関する比較文化的な情報を学び、トータルな国際人としての素養を身につけることに貢献できれば、著者として、これ以上の喜びはありません。

著者一同

本書の使い方

□本書の構成

各章 4 ページで、15 章で構成されています。

□本書の 6 大特長

その 1　法律に関する興味深い情報を、英語で分かりやすく解説しています。

その 2　パッセージに対する語句注を充実させています。

その 3　総合的に英語 4 技能を高めるために、多彩な練習問題を設定しています。

その 4　Vocabulary では 6 つの重要語、Grammar では 3 つの重要項目をパッセージから取り出し、設問しています。

その 5　Comprehension と Composition は、それぞれ 2 段階と 3 段階にレベル設定をしています。

その 6　半期用にも、通年用（TM に補足問題［小テスト、中間／期末テスト］と Task がある）にも利用できます。

□各章のページ構成

<table>
<tr><td rowspan="3">1 ページ目
〜
2 ページ目</td><td>Passage</td><td colspan="2">400 語程度の英文パッセージ。</td></tr>
<tr><td>Words & Phrases</td><td colspan="2">重要な専門語や固有名詞、比較的レベルの高い単語・熟語などに関する注。</td></tr>
<tr><td>Tips</td><td colspan="2">章のテーマに関するおもしろコラム。</td></tr>
<tr><td rowspan="3">3 ページ目</td><td>Vocabulary</td><td colspan="2">全 3 問で、各問重要単語 2 つを 6 つの語（句）から選ぶ。</td></tr>
<tr><td rowspan="2">Comprehension</td><td>A</td><td>英語による内容把握の設問 2 問、4 択式。</td></tr>
<tr><td>B</td><td>英語による内容把握の設問 2 問。
設問リスニング穴埋め式による英問英答問題。</td></tr>
<tr><td rowspan="5">4 ページ目</td><td rowspan="2">Grammar</td><td colspan="2">文法問題 3 問。4 択式。テーマ別。</td></tr>
<tr><td>文法のポイント</td><td>3 つのポイント：それぞれ（1 〜 2 行で簡単に説明）文法問題を解く上でのヒント。</td></tr>
<tr><td rowspan="3">Composition</td><td>(1) 並べ替え問題</td><td>日本文に相当する英文を単語の並べ替えで完成させる。</td></tr>
<tr><td>(2) 部分作文問題</td><td>ヒントを参考に日本文に相当する英文を完成させるために単語を埋め込む。</td></tr>
<tr><td>(3) フル作文問題</td><td>ヒント：3 〜 4 個の語（句）を順に用いて日本文を英文に翻訳する。</td></tr>
</table>

目　次

Chapter 1

What's So Free about Freeways?

速度無制限の高速道路，アウトバーン（ドイツ）

世界には色々な高速道路があります。高速道路は英語で freeway ですが、これは free（無料）という意味でしょうか。この章では高速道路の話をします。

02

Expressways are usually known as freeways in a number of countries. Many people mistakenly consider the word "freeway" to have derived from a "free road," a road with no toll for its use. It is true that most freeways in the U.S. are free of charge, but the "free" in "freeway" is said to come from its feature of allowing traffic to flow freely.

A freeway is defined as a road with its outbound and inbound lanes separated by a median. There are also no traffic signals or stop signs and minor roads are passed over by elevated roadways. Therefore, a freeway is a road one can freely drive a car on without worrying about being impeded by the usual traffic-controlling mechanisms.

However, it is also a fact that many expressways do not require the driver to pay a toll. Freeways in the U.S. or Australia, autobahns in Germany, motorways in the U.K., and autostradas in Poland are fundamentally free of charge.

Autoroutes in France are essentially free of charge but since road construction companies are allowed by law to add tolls to roads, drivers are typically charged for the use of such roads. However, because of public demand, many roads remain toll-free. These include expressways in large cities as well as roads near harbors and borders. In some cases, such as with Italy's autostradas, motorists are commonly charged for the use of the roads.

Germany's 13,000 km of autobahns are noted for the fact that there is no speed limit under the law. A driver is essentially free to speed. On the contrary, it is actually dangerous to drive slowly on these freeways. Stopping can result in serious accidents, so stopping is usually prohibited even in cases where the car runs out of gas. This means that drivers are expected to fill up before heading out on the highway. Unexpected occurrences like flat tires are not considered infractions of the autobahn's safety regulations, because these kinds of happenstances are out of the driver's control for the most part.

Speed on autobahns is actually controlled to a certain point, more so in some areas than others. For stretches of roads without specified speed limits, the recommended speed is 130 km/h. For congested places or inclining/declining sections, the speed limit is between 100 and 130 km/h. Moreover, the speed limits for large trucks and buses are 80 km/h and 100 km/h respectively.

Autobahns are designed in order to make them suitable for high speed driving; therefore, the gradient of the road is limited to a 4% incline in principle. With that said, it is still considerably difficult to maintain control of a vehicle once someone attempts speeds nearing or exceeding 300 km/h.

In conclusion, expressways can be dangerous when driving a car too slowly or too fast. As is often said, "everything in moderation." This principle also applies to the world of expressways.

Words and Phrases

toll 通行料 / **outbound lane** 下り線 / **inbound lane** 上り線 / **median** 中央分離帯 / **traffic signal** 交通信号 / **stop sign** 一時停止の標識 / **minor road** (高速道路に対して)一般道路 / **impede** 遅らせる / **autobahn** アウトバーン(ドイツ，オーストリア，スイスの高速道路) / **autostrada** アウトストラーダ(イタリアの高速道路) / **fundamentally** 基本的に / **toll-free** 通行料が無料である / **flat tires** パンク / **infraction** 違反 / **happenstance** 偶然の出来事 / **stretch** まっすぐに伸びている箇所 / **gradient** 勾配 / **everything in moderation** 何事もほどほどに(するのが大切)

Tips

世界の高速道路の制限速度のあれこれ

一般にヨーロッパの高速道路の制限（ドイツを除く）は 130 キロ前後です。違反に対しては厳しく取り締まっています。制限速度 5 %オーバーするだけで捕まります。つまり、7 キロオーバーで違反になります。オランダ、ベルギー、ルクセンブルクおよび韓国は制限速度が 120 キロ、カナダ、オーストラリア、ロシアは 110 キロ、アメリカは州によって異なりますが、65 マイル（105 キロ）とされています。

カナダでは、高速道路のほとんどが無料ですが、新しく建設された道路は元が取れるまで有料、また 2 人以上が車に乗っていなければ走れない車線もあります。オーストラリアでは、制限速度を 5 キロオーバーするだけでも捕まります。また、自家用車の車内で飲食するだけでも罰金の対象となります。

1 VOCABULARY

次の日本語を読み、(　)に当てはまる語を選んで、英訳を完成させなさい。

(1) 高速道路は、中央分離帯で上りと下りに分けられている道です。
A freeway is a road with outbound and inbound (a. 　　　　　　) separated by a (b. 　　　　　　).

lanes　　lines　　median　　meridian　　midway　　paths

(2) 多くの国では高速道路は料金を請求しませんが、日本では無料ではありません。
In many countries, freeways do not require drivers to pay a (a. 　　　　　　), but those in Japan are not free of (b. 　　　　　　).

bill　　charge　　fine　　rate　　toll　　tuition

(3) ドイツの高速道路であるアウトバーンの勾配は、原則として4%に制限されています。
The gradient of the autobahns in Germany is limited to a 4% (a. 　　　　　　) in (b. 　　　　　　).

incline　　principal　　principality　　principle　　section　　sloping

2 COMPREHENSION

A：次の問いの答えとして最も適当なものを選びなさい。

(1) What country is known for having no speed limit under the law?
(A) France　　(B) Germany　　(C) Australia　　(D) U.K.

(2) How fast are drivers allowed to go in congested places or on slopes on German autobahns?
(A) 50 km/h　　(B) 80 km/h
(C) between 50 and 80 km/h　　(D) between 100 and 130 km/h

B：音声を聴きながら(　)内に単語を入れて問いを完成させ、英語で答えなさい。 03 04

(1) Generally speaking, why are cars (　　　　　　) to move so (　　　　　　) through areas while on freeways?

____

(2) Freeways in France are typically NOT free of (　　　　　　). What three kinds of roads (　　　　　　) nothing to use?

____

3 GRAMMAR

次の(　)に当てはまる最も適当な語(句)を(A)～(D)から選びなさい。

(1) (　　　　　　) most freeways in the U.S. are free of charge, but the "free" in "freeway" is said to come from its feature of allowing traffic to flow freely.

(A) It is true of　　(B) It is true that
(C) The truth was whether　　(D) What is the truth

(2) Stopping on freeways can result in serious accidents, so it is usually prohibited even in cases (　　　　　　) the car runs out of gas.

(A) whose　(B) which　(C) where　(D) why

(3) Autobahns are designed in order to (　　　　　　) them suitable for high speed driving.

(A) ask　(B) order　(C) make　(D) want

文法のポイント

(1) 仮主語の it：it は that 以下を表す仮主語。< it is ＋ 形容詞 ＋ that 節>の形式。
(2) 関係副詞 where の先行詞：point や situation などの名詞を先行詞にできる。
(3) 第 5 文型を取る動詞：< make ＋名詞(O)＋形容詞(A)>で「O を A にする」。

4 COMPOSITION

(1) **次の日本語の意味になるように(　)内の語(句)を並べ替えなさい。**
多くの高速道路で、運転手に通行料の支払いを求めないというのは事実です。
It is a fact (don't / the driver / require / that / many expressways) to pay a toll.

____

(2) **次の日本語の意味になるように、ヒントを参考にしながら(　)を埋めなさい。**
多くの人たちは、freeway は「無料の道路」、すなわち通行料なしで使える道路に由来していると誤って考えています。
Many people mistakenly (　　　　　　) (　　　　　　) the word "freeway" is derived (　　　　　　) "free road," a (　　　　　　) requiring no (　　　　　　) for its use.

ヒント：consider that 節「～だと考える」/ be derived from...「…に由来する」

(3) **次の日本語を英語にしなさい。ただし、(　)内の語(句)を順に使い、単語は必要に応じて変化させなさい。**
しばしば言われているように、何事もほどほどが肝心です。この原則は高速道路の世界にも当てはまります。(mentioned; moderation; name; apply)

____

Chapter 2

Riding a Horse While Drunk Is Illegal?

飲酒乗馬の取り締まり（アメリカ）

馬も車と同じで、酒に酔って乗れば違反なのでしょうか？ たとえば、馬を重要な交通手段とすることのあるアメリカで実際にあった話を紹介しましょう。

05

To Americans, horses were an important means of transportation in the past and were held in the same esteem then as cars are at present. Even now some Americans hold horses in high regard in terms of convenience in certain situations.

On September 9, 2013, in Boulder, Colorado, a severely drunken 45-year-old man, who was riding a horse, was placed in custody for some time on suspicion of drunken horseback riding and obstructing traffic.

The inebriated fellow was on his way to his brother's wedding ceremony held in Utah, about 965 km away. When the police stopped and searched the man who was obviously intoxicated, a small pistol and some cans of beer were found in one of his bags and, in another bag, a dog.

This incident is quite American. And the fact that he was not held accountable for possession of a handgun is also typical of the way things are done in the U.S. After all, Americans are allowed to carry a firearm if it is properly licensed. Late on the evening of the same day as his arrest, he was released and resumed his journey to the ceremony on horseback. He had told authorities the reason why he was riding a horse was because he was missing his driver's license.

In Australia, a man who was speaking on his mobile phone while driving a horse-pulled wagon was ticketed and had to pay a fine of 250 Australian dollars (about 20,000 yen). The violator was astonished because the cart was moving at a very slow speed of two kilometers per hour, a speed that didn't seem to be dangerous for phone use. Besides that, he had never been ticketed for this reason in the past.

Unbeknownst to him, in March 2011, the law was changed; the article stating "the use of a mobile phone is prohibited when you drive a motor-driven vehicle" was altered and had the words "motor-driven" omitted.

According to Japan's Road Traffic Law, an article states that nobody must drive a vehicle and the like under the influence of alcohol (Item 1, Article 65). Incidentally, a horse corresponds to a light vehicle lacking a motor, such as a bicycle, a cart, or a vehicle pulled by a human or animal and not placed on a rail. This law implies that a person can't ride a horse or any other light vehicle with alcohol in their system.

Committing the act of driving while drunk, or *sakeyoi-unten*, will result in the offender being subject to up to 5 years' imprisonment or a fine of less than a million yen. With a breath-alcohol level of 0.15mg or less, the driver is considered to be driving under the influence, or *shukiobi-unten*. If a person under the influence is using a light vehicle such as a horse or bicycle, they won't be charged with a crime even though the act of driving a light vehicle while under the influence is technically illegal.

When all is said and done, it's obvious that it is better not to be under the influence of alcohol while doing anything that could result in harm to oneself or others, including driving a car or riding a horse.

Words and Phrases

hold A in the same esteem as... Aを(…と)同じように尊重する / **hold A in high regard** Aを尊重する / **custody** 拘置、留置 / **obstruct** 妨害する / **inebriated** 酔った / **fellow** 男 / **intoxicated** 酔っている / **horse-pulled wagon** 馬車 / **ticket** 違反切符を切る / **fine** 罰金 / **violator** 違反者 / **unbeknownst to A** Aが知らない間に / **motor-driven** モーターで駆動する / **correspond to...** …に相当する / **light vehicle** 軽車両 / **imprisonment** 懲役 / **breath-alcohol level** 呼気中アルコール濃度(現在は 0.3mg 以上が酒気帯運転) / **when all is said and done** 結局

Tips

馬にまつわる表現

アメリカ人にとって馬は今でも重要な地域があり、歴史上、人間と馬は切り離せない関係があります。だから、Phillip さんという名前が存在するのです。Phillip は< Phil + hippo >から来ており、phil は「好き」で hippo は「馬」だから、Phillip とは「馬好き」という意味になります。このように人名になるほど、馬好きが多かったということがうかがえます。

hippo が「馬」の意味であるのは、hippopotamus(河馬)という単語を分析すれば分かります。hippo は「馬」で、potam は「河」となります。potam が河であるのは、Mesopotamia(meso[中] + potam[河] + ia[地]→チグリス川とユーフラテス川の間の土地=メソポタミア)という単語に現れていることからも分かるでしょう。

1 VOCABULARY

次の日本語を読み、（　）に当てはまる語を選んで、英訳を完成させなさい。

(1) 過去に交通手段として利用された馬は、現在の車と同じくらい尊重されていました。
Horses used as a means of transportation in the past were held in the same (a.　　　　　) then as cars are at (b.　　　　　).

estate　esteem　presence　present　presentation　status

(2) その45才の男は、飲酒乗馬の疑いで、少しの間、拘置されていました。
The 45-year-old man was placed in (a.　　　　　) for some time on (b.　　　　　) of riding a horse while drunk.

courtesy　cruelty　custody　suspense　suspension　suspicion

(3) 飲酒乗馬が原因で警察に逮捕された男は、釈放されて結婚式の場所まで、長い道のりの乗馬の旅を再開しました。
The man arrested by the police due to his drunken horseback riding was (a.　　　　　) and (b.　　　　　) his long trip to the wedding ceremony on horseback.

recalled　released　relieved　resumed　retreated　retrieved

2 COMPREHENSION

A：次の問いの答えとして最も適当なものを選びなさい。

(1) Where was a severely drunken 45-year-old man arrested?
(A) Australia　(B) Japan　(C) Colorado, U.S.　(D) Utah, U.S.

(2) After his arrest, when did the man set out for his brother's wedding ceremony?
(A) On Sept. 8　(B) On Sept. 9　(C) On Sept. 10　(D) On Sept. 11

B：音声を聴きながら（　）内に単語を入れて問いを完成させ、英語で答えなさい。 06 07

(1) What are the two reasons why the man (　　　　　) was driving a wagon was astonished when he was (　　　　　)?

____

(2) What does Japan's Road Traffic Law say (　　　　　) (　　　　　) driving?

____

3 GRAMMAR

次の(　)に当てはまる最も適当な語(句)を(A)～(D)から選びなさい。

(1) A man traveling with two bags was arrested. The police found a small pistol and some cans of beer in one of his bags, and a dog in (　　　　　　).

(A) other　(B) another　(C) the other　(D) the others

(2) The fact (　　　　　　) he was not charged with possession of a handgun may be strange from a Japanese perspective.

(A) where　(B) of　(C) that　(D) which

(3) He told the police (　　　　　　) he was riding a horse was because his driver's license was missing.

(A) reason　(B) what　(C) the reason　(D) why

文法のポイント

(1) 2者・2物間の数え方：最初の1つ目は one、残りの1つは the other となる。
(2) 同格の that：<特定の名詞＋ that ＋完全文>の形。その場合 that は接続詞。
(3) 関係副詞 why の省略：the reason why の代わりに the reason that が好まれる傾向にあり、これらの why や that は省略することも可能。

4 COMPOSITION

(1) 次の日本語の意味になるように(　)内の語(句)を並べ替えなさい。

オーストラリアでは、馬が引くワゴンを運転している間に、携帯電話で話をした人が違反切符を切られました。

In Australia, (who / mobile phone / was / a man / speaking / his / on) while driving a horse-pulled wagon was ticketed.

____

(2) 次の日本語の意味になるように、ヒントを参考にしながら(　)を埋めなさい。

この法律は、飲酒した状態で馬や他の軽車両に乗ってはいけないということを意味しています。

This law (　　　　　　) (　　　　　　) a person can't ride a horse or (　　　　　　) light vehicles when he or (　　　　　　) is (　　　　　　) the influence of alcohol.

ヒント：imply「～を意味する」/ under the influence of alcohol「飲酒の状態で」

(3) 次の日本語を英語にしなさい。ただし、(　)内の語(句)を順に使い、単語は必要に応じて変化させなさい。

「モーター付きの乗り物を運転中に、携帯電話の使用を禁止する」という条項から「モーター付きの」という文言が削除されました。(prohibit; motor-driven; delete)

____

Chapter 3

Walk Your Dog Three Times a Day!

犬は１日３回，散歩させなければならない（イタリア）

日本では、犬は１日２回散歩させることが多いですね。どうもイタリアでは３回散歩させることが義務のようです。その理由は何であるか考えてみましょう。

08

In Japan, a snowman is made up of two snowballs, while in the West, it consists of three balls, representing a head, torso and base which serves as legs. Before entering a room, people usually knock twice in Japan, whereas in the West, they do it three times. Westerners, however, often knock twice on a bathroom stall's door. This means knocking twice is used to politely check whether a room is vacant or not, and knocking three times is to check whether it is OK to actually enter a room.

Regarding various acts, especially those we take for granted, "two for Japan and three for the West" may be a general rule to keep in mind. The same can be said about walking dogs. In Japan, people usually walk their dogs twice a day, in the morning and in the evening; however, in the West, they do this three times in many cases.

In Turin, Italy, a law was enacted that forces people to walk their dogs three times a day. Turin is famous for hosting the Juventus Football Club, which has won the Serie A championship 27 times. Turin is also the fourth largest city in Italy with a population of about 1.7 million, the top 3 being Rome, Milan and Naples. It became a sister city of Nagoya, Japan, in May, 2005.

According to the law, if you don't walk your dog three times a day, you will be fined 500 Euro, or about 80,000 yen. Walking dogs while riding a bicycle and forcing a dog to cruelly exert itself is also illegal. Cutting dogs' tails and dyeing their hair also entail strict repercussions. This may remind some of the animal protection ordinances issued by Shogun Tokugawa Tsunayoshi in Japan.

There is a serious reason behind this law: 150,000 dogs and 200,000 cats are discarded every year in Italy. Therefore, this law was enforced in Turin in 2005 to seek to improve the treatment of domesticated animals and cut back on the amount of strays.

It is distressing for vacationers to see people abandoning their pets in parking lots or tossing them to the sides of freeways while touring Italy. Shockingly, 60,000 dogs were abandoned during a three-month period in one summer.

On the other hand, the total number of dogs and cats that are euthanized at Japan's public health centers in a year is said to be more than 400,000, so Japanese cannot criticize the Italian situation. However, considering the fact that Italy's population is half that of Japan, the number is still significant.

Recently, police have been paying more attention to this tragic habit and the number of dogs being abandoned on or near freeways is decreasing. Unfortunately though, there has been an increase in the number of dogs being discarded in the countryside away from the prying eyes of the police in the cities. One thing is for sure, owners of pets, regardless of nationality, should be responsible for the health and well-being of their animals.

Words and Phrases

snowman 雪だるま / **represent** 表す / **torso** 胴 / **base** 土台 / **bathroom stall** トイレの個室 / **vacant** 空室である / **take A for granted** Aを当然と思う / **Turin** トリノ（イタリアの都市）/ **Milan** ミラノ / **Naples** ナポリ / **cruelly** 無慈悲に / **entail** （必然的に）～を伴う / **strict** 厳しい / **repercussion** 影響 / **ordinance** 布告（=「お触れ」）、条例 / **discard** 捨てる / **domesticated animal** 家畜 / **cut back on...** …を減らす / **stray** 迷った動物 / **euthanize** 安楽死させる / **significant** 相当数の / **prying** じろじろ見る / **well-being** 幸福な状態

Tips

生類憐みの令は必ずしも悪法とは言えない!?

生類憐みの令という名の法律があったわけではありません。これは、江戸幕府五代将軍綱吉が出した「お触れ」を総称したものです。綱吉は丙戌（ひのえいぬ）年生まれで、無類の犬好きであったため、犬のみが対象とされていたように思われていますが、それは間違いです。猫や鳥、魚や貝、虫など、更には、人間の幼児や老人までがその対象でした。牛馬の遺棄の禁止や捨て子や病人の保護まで扱われました。

しかし、1696年に犬虐待の密告者に賞金が支払われるようになったことがきっかけで、監視社会となったので、悪法のように思われています。でも、実際には生物をいたわる精神論を高める上で貢献したと言えるでしょう。また、日本人には殺生を厳しく禁じましたが、中国人とオランダ人に対しては、例外として豚や鶏を食べることを許していました。

1 VOCABULARY

次の日本語を読み、（　）に当てはまる語を選んで、英訳を完成させなさい。

1. トリノでは犬の扱いに関して従わなければならない法律があります。たとえば、犬の毛を染めると、その反響は厳しいものとなるでしょう。
There are certain rules which must be followed regarding the treatment of dogs in Turin; for example, (a. 　　　　　　　　) their hair will result in strict (b. 　　　　　　　　).

dicing　dyeing　dying　repellents　repentance　repercussions

2. 残念なことに、休日の行楽客は、人々が高速道路のサービスエリアの駐車場に、ペットを置き去りにしているのをよく目の当たりにします。
Unfortunately, (a. 　　　　　　　　) often see people (b. 　　　　　　　　) their pets in the parking lots of freeway service areas.

abandoning　annulling　deleting　friends　troublemakers　vacationers

3. 日本で安楽死させられる犬と猫の総数は、年間 40 万匹以上と言われているので、日本人はイタリアの状況を批判できません。
Since the total number of dogs and cats that are (a. 　　　　　　　　) in Japan is said to be over 400,000 a year, Japanese cannot (b. 　　　　　　　　) the Italian situation.

criticize　eulogized　euphonized　euthanized　improve　praise

2 COMPREHENSION

A：次の問いの答えとして最も適当なものを選びなさい。

(1) How many times do Westerners knock on a bathroom stall's door?
(A) once　(B) twice　(C) three times　(D) four times

(2) In Italy, what city became a sister city of Nagoya, Japan?
(A) Milan　(B) Naples　(C) Rome　(D) Turin

B：音声を聴きながら（　）内に単語を入れて問いを完成させ、英語で答えなさい。　09 10

(1) What situation (　　　　　　　　) to the law requiring people to (　　　　　　　　) their dogs three times a day?

____

(2) How many dogs are (　　　　　　　　) (　　　　　　　　) during the summer in Italy?

____

3 GRAMMAR

次の(　)に当てはまる最も適当な語(句)を(A)〜(D)から選びなさい。

(1) In Japan, people usually walk their dog twice (　　　　　　) day, in the morning and in the evening.

(A) one　　(B) the　　(C) the whole　　(D) per

(2) A law was enacted that (　　　　　　) people walk their dog three times a day.

(A) asks　　(B) forces　　(C) makes　　(D) wants

(3) Considering the fact that Italy's population is half (　　　　　　) of Japan, the number is still significant.

(A) this　　(B) that　　(C) those　　(D) these

文法のポイント

(1) 冠詞 a / an：「〜につき」の意味になる用法がある。per で置き換え可能。
(2) 使役動詞 make：＜ make ＋ O ＋ do ＞という形。「O に〜させる」という意味。
(3) 代名詞 that：この that は前出の単数名詞を受ける。複数名詞は those で受ける。

4 COMPOSITION

(1) **次の日本語の意味になるように(　)内の語(句)を並べ替えなさい。**

最近、警察はこの痛ましい習慣に、さらに注意を払うようになっています。

Police (attention / this tragic habit / are / to / paying / more) these days.

____

(2) **次の日本語の意味になるように、ヒントを参考にしながら(　)を埋めなさい。**

2回のノックは空室であるかどうかの確認、3回のノックは実際に入室可能かどうかを確認するために用いられるとする説があります。

There is a (　　　　　　) that says a person knocks twice to check whether (　　　　　　) (　　　　　　) a room is vacant and (　　　　　　) three (　　　　　　) (　　　　　　) check whether it is OK to (　　　　　　) enter a room.

ヒント：a theory that...「…という説」/ whether or not「〜かどうか」

(3) **次の日本語を英語にしなさい。ただし、(　)内の語(句)を順に使い、単語は必要に応じて変化させなさい。**

国籍に関わらず、ペットの飼い主は、ペットが他人に迷惑をかけないよう注意することに加え、ペットの健康状態に責任を持たなければなりません。(regardless; careful; trouble; responsible)

____

Chapter 4

Hungary Introduces a Tax on Chips

健康のためのポテトチップス税（ハンガリー）

ポテトチップスが大好きな人も多いと思います。もし、これに高い税金がかかったらどうしますか？こんなユニークな税を導入した国を紹介します。

08

People who live in Hungary may actually be hungry and quite possibly angry. In fact, the Hungarian government introduced a 'fat tax,' a special tax on foods with high fat, salt and sugar content. This means that people could expect to pay more than usual for consuming greater quantities of unhealthy foods.

The 10-forint (roughly $0.05) tax was implemented on September 1, 2011, as the government's way to encourage its population to eat healthily. With a solid two-thirds of the Hungarian populace categorized as overweight or obese, this tax was formed not only to combat unhealthy diets but also to help fund the country's underfinanced health system.

Lisa McCooey, director of communications for FoodDrinkEurope, explained that it is a tax on products with high sugar, salt or caffeine. According to her, taxable products include soft drinks with added sugar, energy drinks with added sugar and caffeine, prepackaged sweetened products, salty snacks, high salt content condiments, soup mixes, gravy mixes, and bases.

With the idea built on good intentions, the experimental law was left to stand the test of time, but the results were quite unexpected—and not necessarily to everyone's satisfaction.

After 18 months of observation, it was found that consumption of the taxed food dropped significantly, but the people also found themselves buying less of all kinds of food. With Hungarians already spending 17% of their income on food alone, the tax led to them spending an additional 25% on most food and drinks—one of the highest rates within the European Union. This put a large strain on the populace, especially those in the lower-income bracket, who depended on cheap prepackaged food.

Food manufacturers also tried skirting the tax by modifying their products to include less salt and sugar, and thus, while people bought less of the taxable food, they still had access to cheaper, and still unhealthy, alternatives. Everyone avoided the tax like the plague, but in the end, consumers suffered as businesses tried to distribute prices among all their products, introducing inflation that made everyone fail to feel the impact of the special tax in the midst of increased food prices. Thus, the tax resulted in people paying roughly 25% more on food.

While many critics have soured on the law, others also saw the inherent advantages brought about by the special 'fat tax.'

First, with the burden of the tax falling on the people, the targeted 'obese' population was forced to stop eating the now-expensive, unhealthy food. The only way to get these foodstuffs was to work harder to afford them.

Second, with several products modified to fit the standards of non-taxable food, the end product became significantly less "unhealthy," which in turn had a considerable impact on the health of the people, whether they noticed or not.

Third, the government was able to collect 17 billion forints from the tax, though the figures were nearly 3 billion forints less than the anticipated amount. The special tax still worked, even though it caused an unsavory ripple effect on the market as a whole.

Other neighboring countries, including Denmark and France, have tried—and failed—to implement similar 'fat taxes.' Hungary has persevered, instead choosing to stand firm as the rest of the world watches them closely. If the 'fat tax' does prove to be largely beneficial in the long run, the rest of the world is sure to follow. After all, "If they can do it, why can't we?"

Words and Phrases

content 含有量 / **forint** フォリント（ハンガリーの通貨単位） / **implement** 施行する / **solid** 完全な、正味の / **populace** 民衆 / **obese** 肥満の / **underfinanced** 資金不足の / **condiments** 薬味・香辛料 / **put a large strain on...** …に多大な負担をかける / **the lower-income bracket** 低所得層 / **prepackaged** あらかじめ包装された（すぐに販売できる） / **skirt** 回避する / **modify** 変更する / **plague** 疫病・災難 / **sour on...** …に幻滅する / **now-expensive** 今はもう高価になった / **non-taxable** 非課税の / **anticipated** 予期された / **unsavory** 芳しくない / **cause a ripple effect** 波紋を投じる

Tips

世界の面白い税金

ヒゲ税：ロシアで昔、採用されたもので、ヒゲをはやしている人への課税です。

空気税：18 世紀、ルイ 15 世時代のフランスで空気を吸う人に課税。ある意味平等な税ですね。

渋滞税：イギリスのロンドンで、平日午前 7 時から午後 6 時半にロンドンの特定のエリアに侵入すると課税されるしくみになっています。

光るおもちゃ税：

激しく発光したり、火花が出るおもちゃ（銃のおもちゃや花火など）に課税。銃犯罪の低下にひと役買っていると言われるアメリカ、ウェストバージニア州の税です。

1 VOCABULARY

次の日本語を読み、(　)に当てはまる語を選んで、英訳を完成させなさい。

(1) 太り過ぎに分類される人は、不健康な食品を大量に摂っている傾向があります。
People who are (a. 　　　　　　) as overweight tend to (b. 　　　　　　) greater quantities of unhealthy food.

assume　categorized　consume　dramatized　resume　symbolized

(2) 善良な意図に基づいた論理的思考によって、その人々による健康的な生き方の追求が確実になりました。
Using logic based on good (a. 　　　　　　) has ensured the (b. 　　　　　　) of a healthy lifestyle by the people.

conservation　contention　inflation　intentions　plague　pursuit

(3) 肥満税導入は、ハンガリー人の生き方に有益な影響を相当与えたようです。
The introduction of the "fat tax" seems to have had a (a. 　　　　　　) (b. 　　　　　　) impact on the way Hungarians live.

beneficial　benevolent　considerably　considerate　repectfully　respectively

2 COMPREHENSION

A: 次の問いの答えとして最も適当なものを選びなさい。

(1) What proportion of the Hungarians is regarded as overweight or obese?
(A) 2/3　(B) 1/10　(C) 17 percent　(D) 25 percent

(2) Which of the items below is NOT a taxable product?
(A) soft drinks containing sugar　(B) salty energy drinks
(C) high salt-content condiments　(D) gravy mixes

B：音声を聴きながら(　)内に単語を入れて問いを完成させ、英語で答えなさい。 12 13

(1) There are two (　　　　　　) for the tax introduction: One is to (　　　　　　) the problem of the unhealthy (　　　　　　) of Hungarians. What is the other?

____

(2) What was the last (　　　　　　) of the tax mentioned by the (　　　　　　)?

____

3 GRAMMAR

次の(　)に当てはまる最も適当な語(句)を(A)～(D)から選びなさい。

(1) Those (　　　　　　) live in Hungary may be troubled by the “fat tax.”

(A) who　(B) whom　(C) whose　(D) which

(2) It was discovered (　　　　　　) food manufacturers tried to avoid producing taxable foods.

(A) what　(B) where　(C) that　(D) to do

(3) With the new tax (　　　　　　) on unhealthy foods, Hungary planned to solve their nation's health problem and financial issues.

(A) impose　(B) imposing　(C) imposed　(D) to impose

文法のポイント

(1) 関係代名詞：直後に動詞が来る場合は、主格の関係代名詞を用いる。先行詞が人なら who、人以外なら which を用いる。

(2) 形式主語構文：< it is ... to do ～> や < it is ... that ～> のような構文。it は to do ～や that ～を指す。「...」の箇所に動詞の過去分詞が来ることが多い。

(3) 付帯状況の with：< with+O+C >の形で「O が C の状況で」という意味を表す。C は、形容詞、副詞、doing、-ed または前置詞句。

4 COMPOSITION

(1) 次の日本語の意味になるように(　)内の語(句)を並べ替えなさい。

新たに導入された税制は、その市民に大きなストレスを与えました。

The newly introduced tax system (a / the / on / strain / large / put) citizens.

____

(2) 次の日本語の意味になるように、ヒントを参考にしながら(　)を埋めなさい。

政府は税から 170 億フォリントを集めることができました。数値は予期した額より 30 億フォリント近くも少なかったのですが…。

The government was able to (　　　　　　)(　　　　　　)(　　　　　　) forints from the tax, though the figures were almost 3 billion forints (　　　　　　)(　　　　　　)(　　　　　　)(　　　　　　)(　　　　　　).

ヒント：10 億＝ one billion / …よりも～だけ少ない＝～ less than...

(3) 次の日本語を英語にしなさい。ただし、(　)内の語(句)を順に使い、単語は必要に応じて変化させなさい。

その法律について幻滅した批評家は多い一方で、固有の利点がその税によりもたらされたと見る批評家もいました。(sour; inherent; bring about)

____

Chapter 5 Don't Tie Alligators to Fire Hydrants!

「ワニを消火栓につなぐな」とはどういうこと？（アメリカ）

ワニが生息していないのに「ワニを消火栓につないではならない」という法律があるとの噂です。「犬を消火栓につなぐな」なら分かる気もしますが…。

14

There are many stories of peculiar laws floating around on the Internet, shared between people through social networking and e-mail. While most are nothing but urban myths, many are quite hilarious. Some are rooted in truth, being exaggerations of existing laws. When real laws are taken out of context or misinterpreted, things can become silly. Such is the case with a strange little law in Detroit, Michigan, USA, that reads: "Alligators may not be tied to fire hydrants."

In the first place, this law may throw people off and seem like a hoax simply because alligators don't live in Michigan, a state where the weather is too cold for them to survive. The possibility of people raising alligators as pets is plausible. However, with all the permits required as well as space and care needed for the pet, it seems unfeasible. From a common sense standpoint, this law seems ridiculous. So where does this law really come from?

Web sources are often incomplete and unreliable, but in the case of this law there is a book which shines some light on the idea of tying alligators to fire hydrants. *You May Not Tie an Alligator to a Fire Hydrant: 101 Real Dumb Laws*, published in 2002, was written by two high school students, Jeff Koon and Andy Powell, who previously had been debating such laws on a website. The book cites many unusual laws from the US, especially from the South. The law regarding alligators and hydrants provided the book its catchy title.

The two authors researched the topic and found that this law is considered by folks to have originated in New Orleans, Louisiana. There was no evidence found that the law actually came from New Orleans, though. They were, however, able to discover a law in Michigan which sounds a lot like the law in question. There is actually a law which prohibits people from tying animals to fire hydrants, but it does not mention alligators. A local ordinance in Detroit states: "No person shall in any manner obstruct the use of any fire hydrant in the city, or have, place or allow to be placed any material or thing in front thereof, or connect or tie thereto any object, animal or thing."

This means that the statement "Alligators may not be tied to fire hydrants" is true. Though, it's just as true that you are not allowed to tie a dog, a chicken or an elephant to a fire hydrant. Had the law been misinterpreted as "Dogs may not be tied to fire hydrants," it would gain no traction. It certainly wouldn't wind up as a fun little piece of trivia to tell a friend.

In all seriousness, this law actually aims to ensure that in case of fire, there is no object or living creature obstructing a fire hydrant and impeding firefighters. Not being able to use the hydrant may result in tragic consequences.

All in all, "Alligators may not be tied to fire hydrants" is an excellent example of a law that is rooted in truth but has been warped to the point of hilarity. All that was needed was to add an exotic animal. The human tendency to remark upon things comic or idiotic did the rest.

Words and Phrases

peculiar 風変りの / **nothing but** ～に過ぎない / **urban myths** 都市伝説 / **hilarious** 滑稽な / **rooted in...** …に基づいている / **misinterpret** 誤解する / **fire hydrant** 消火栓 / **hoax** 作り話 / **plausible** もっともらしい / **unfeasible** 実行不可能な / **cite** 引用する / **gain no traction** 注目されない / **wind up** 終わる / **trivia** 雑学的知識 / **in all seriousness** 冗談抜きで / **impede** 遅らせる / **all in all** 結局のところ / **warped to...** …にまでゆがめられた / **hilarity** 滑稽

Tips

各州で法律が異なるアメリカ

アメリカでは州ごとにかなり特色のある法律が施行されています。アメリカを 1 つの国として考えるよりも、各州が別々の国で、EU のような共同体としてアメリカという国家が存在すると考えた方が合理的です。

たとえば、飲酒運転（DUI: Driving Under Influence）に関して、連邦法では、各州に対して罰則を加重する法を制定するよう方向性を示しており、具体的な規定については、各州で定めることになっています。

1 VOCABULARY

次の日本語を読み、（　）に当てはまる語を選んで、英訳を完成させなさい。

(1) SNSで共有された一連の法律は、都市伝説にすぎません。
A series of laws shared by social network services is (*a.*) but an urban (*b.*).

anything　everything　mess　miss　myth　nothing

(2) ワニを育てることはあり得る話に思えるが、条例の規制により不可能です。
It may sound (*a.*) to raise an alligator at home; however, it is (*b.*) due to it violating local ordinances.

admirable　desirable　feasible　incorrect　plausible　unfeasible

(3) 差し迫った危機の際は、消火栓の邪魔になっているものはすべて撤去します。
Any objects (*a.*) fire hydrants will be removed in case of (*b.*) crises.

constructing　depending　destructing　impending　insisting　obstructing

2 COMPREHENSION

A：次の問いの答えとして最も適当なものを選びなさい。

(1) Why is the law in Detroit funny?
(A) The weather is too hot.
(B) It was enforced in New Orleans.
(C) The law doesn't make sense.
(D) Alligators don't live there.

(2) When Jeff and Andy wrote *You May Not Tie an Alligator to a Fire Hydrant: 101 Real Dumb Laws*, what were they?
(A) High school students
(B) Firefighters
(C) Novelists
(D) Alligator hunters

B：音声を聴きながら（　）内に単語を入れて問いを完成させ、英語で答えなさい。 15 16

(1) Where did Jeff and Andy find a law ( ) to the one in ( )?

____

(2) What is really ( ) in the ( ) "Alligators may not be ( ) to fire hydrants"?

____

3 GRAMMAR

次の(　)に当てはまる最も適当な語(句)を(A)～(D)から選びなさい。

(1) Most are (　　　　　　) urban myths, but many of them are quite funny.

(A) almost all　(B) the only　(C) nothing but　(D) not more

(2) The weather is (　　　　　　) cold that they can not survive.

(A) pretty　(B) so　(C) too　(D) very

(3) There is a law (　　　　　　) people from tying animals to fire hydrants.

(A) prohibit　(B) prohibits　(C) prohibiting　(D) prohibited

文法のポイント

(1) -thing but の表現：anything but（～どころではない）と nothing but（～にすぎない）の2つが重要。

(2) ＜too ~ to do...＞の表現：「…するには～すぎる」「とても～なので…できない」という意味。＜so ~ that...cannot V＞で書き換えることが可能。

(3) ＜There+be+A+分詞＞の構造：A に後続する分詞は、「A が～する」という能動関係であれば現在分詞、「A が～される」という受動関係であれば過去分詞となる。

4 COMPOSITION

(1) 次の日本語の意味になるように(　)内の語(句)を並べ替えなさい。

人々がワニをペットとして飼うことはあり得ます。

The possibility (alligators / people / as / keeping / pets / of) is plausible.

____

(2) 次の日本語の意味になるように、ヒントを参考にしながら(　)を埋めなさい。

その法律が“犬を消火栓につないではいけない”と誤解されていたなら、今は注目を浴びていないでしょう。

If the law (　　　　　　) (　　　　　　) misinterpreted as “Dogs (　　　　　　) not be tied to fire hydrants,” it (　　　　　　) not (　　　　　　) traction.

ヒント：misinterpret A as B「A を B と誤解する」/ gain traction「注目を浴びる」

(3) 次の日本語を英語にしなさい。ただし、(　)内の語(句)を順に使い、単語は必要に応じて変化させなさい。

インターネット上では一風変わった法律について、あまりにたくさんの話があるので、いくつかは都市伝説であるかもしれません。(stories; peculiar; myths)

____

Chapter 6

Marriage and Divorce in Different Cultures

４回続けて同じ人と結婚できない？（イスラム）

残念なことに結婚に離婚がつきものですが、結婚観・離婚観は、国や宗教により異なります。この章では、主としてイスラム圏の事情を学びましょう。

17

Divorce laws vary greatly from one religion to another. There are some religions which don't officially allow the dissolution of marriage, such as Roman Catholicism, while other religions accept it, even if they don't encourage separation.

Islam is one of the religions which accept divorce, although it has strict guidelines regarding this subject. A divorce initiated by a man is called "*talāq*" and can be easily obtained, while a divorce requested by a woman is called "*khula*" and is usually harder to obtain. Sunni Muslims require a waiting period of three months ("*iddah*") during which the couple is encouraged to reconcile, especially if it is discovered that the woman is pregnant. During *iddah*, the woman cannot marry another man and she continues to live in the house of her husband.

While all of the above is straightforward enough, there is a regulation affecting those living under Sharia Law which falls under the category of being a funny law: A woman who has divorced three times from her husband cannot re-marry him unless she marries another man and divorces him, or he dies. At the same time, the *iddah* period must be respected before divorcing the second man. This law is called Nikah Halala. At first glance, it is hard to see the reasoning behind this actual law. In order to gain full comprehension of its intricacies, one must first understand Islam and the way Muslims think.

A woman who has divorced three times from the same man assumes the burden of being a "*harām*"(sin) for her former husband. There are certain conditions of marriage required in Islam. It is considered that there is wisdom behind every rule of Islam, and so it is in the case of this decree. The matter of divorce is taken seriously by Islamic scholars and rules like this one represent a last resort for couples with potentially irreconcilable problems. It is hard to imagine that a fourth marriage taking place directly after the third would be considered wise.

This rule is stated in the Quran in Sura 2-228-232. It is also important to mention that the fourth marriage of the woman must be genuine and based on honest intentions. Islam does not encourage schemes such as allowing a woman to marry another man solely as a stepping stone in order to be able to lawfully re-marry her former husband. This simply means that Nikah Halala cannot be planned in advance. Muslim scholars say that this law aims to decrease the occurrence of three divorces and to protect the honor of women.

It is said that there is a similarly complex edict in the American state of Kentucky which states that it is illegal to marry the same person a fourth time, but there is no evidence that this is true. If there is such a law, its purpose is to probably suggest people take matters of divorce seriously. Either way, such a situation is less likely to happen in an American state than in an Islamic one. Muslim husbands can divorce by repeating to their wives, "I divorce you," three times in a row. This tradition bypasses any of the legal issues we'd see in countries like the United States and makes separation much easier.

Amusing anecdotes like this one show us that views on marriage differ significantly in various cultures and religions in the world. We also learn that laws that were conceived centuries ago based on religion are sometimes the most difficult to understand and explain.

Words and Phrases

vary from one A to another Aによって異なる / **dissolution** 解消 / **Roman Catholicism** ローマカトリック教 / **separation**（文脈から）離婚 / **Sunni Muslims** スンニ派のイスラム教徒 / **reconcile** 和解する / **pregnant** 妊娠している / **straightforward** 分かりやすい / **regulation** 規定 / **Sharia Law** イスラム法 / **intricacies** 複雑な事情 / **burden** 重荷 / **decree** 法令 / **irreconcilable** 和解できない / **Quran** コーラン（=Koran）/ **scheme** 企み / **edict** 法令 / **in a row** 続けて / **bypass** 無視する / **anecdote** 逸話

Tips

結婚と離婚の法律

男女を取り巻く法律は非常に多く存在します。なかでも結婚と離婚に関するものは宗教色や慣習色が強いものも少なくありません。結婚と離婚は法的行為ですから、それなりの制約があってもおかしくありません。

しかし、独身税があると聞いたら驚くことでしょう。ブルガリアには20歳以上の男女が所得に応じ独身税を払わなければならないという法律があります。正確に言うと「ありました」となります。少子化を危惧した政府が苦肉の策として導入した独身税ですが、反対意見が続出したことと効果が期待値を下回ったことで廃止されました。

1 VOCABULARY

次の日本語を読み、（　）に当てはまる語を選んで、英訳を完成させなさい。

(1) ある国で結婚の解消が禁止であるということは、ただあまり知られていない話です。
That the (a.) of marriage is prohibited in a country is nothing but an (b.).

analects　anecdote　anthology　delusion　desolation　dissolution

(2) ある地域では男性が愛する女性を誘拐して結婚することも適切だとみなされているという事実は容易には理解できません。しかし、これはまさに伝統文化の複雑な事情を反映しています。
It's tough to gain full (a.) of the fact that in some places it is considered appropriate for a man to abduct a single woman he loves and marry her, but this does reflect on the (b.) of traditional cultures.

apprehension　comprehension　intricacies　intrinsic　intrusive　understand

(3) トムは行政からの複雑な命令を避けるため、妻と和解しました。
Tom (a.) with his wife in order to bypass a strict and complex government (b.) issued recently.

edict　edition　eviction　reconciled　relaxed　retracted

2 COMPREHENSION

A：次の問いの答えとして最も適当なものを選びなさい。

(1) According to Muslim scholars, what is the purpose of Nikah Halala?

(A) To be planned in advance　(B) To increase the population
(C) To protect human rights　(D) To protect the honor of women

(2) How many times is it illegal to marry the same person in Kentucky?

(A) once　(B) twice　(C) three times　(D) four times

B：音声を聴きながら（　）内に単語を入れて問いを完成させ、英語で答えなさい。 18 19

(1) What is a woman ( ) ( ) doing during the *iddah*?

____

(2) According to the Islamic ( ), in what case can a woman who has ( ) three times ( ) her ex-husband?

____

3 GRAMMAR

次の（　）に当てはまる最も適当な語（句）を（A）〜（D）から選びなさい。

(1) Islam is one of the religions that accept divorce; (　　　　　　　　), it has strict guidelines regarding this subject.

(A) however　　(B) yet　　(C) therefore　　(D) besides

(2) (　　　　　　　　) gain full comprehension of its intricacies, one must first understand Islam and the way Muslims think.

(A) Owing　　(B) So as　　(C) So as to　　(D) In order that

(3) Islam does not encourage schemes such as (　　　　　　　　) a woman marry another man solely as a stepping stone.

(A) let　　(B) allow　　(C) letting　　(D) allowed

文法のポイント

(1) 逆接の接続副詞：however や nevertheless、notwithstanding などがある。
(2) 目的を表す表現：< in order to do >や< so as to do >などがある。
(3) 使役動詞 let：< let+O+do >の形。< allow+O+to do >で置き換え可能。

4 COMPOSITION

(1) 次の日本語の意味になるように（　）内の語（句）を並べ替えなさい。

正式には結婚の解消を許可していない宗教もいくつかあります。

There are (the dissolution / some religions / that / of / officially / allow / don't) marriage.

____

(2) 次の日本語の意味になるように、ヒントを参考にしながら（　）を埋めなさい。

そのような状況は、アメリカよりもイスラム国家の方がはるかに起こりやすい傾向にあります。

Such a situation is (　　　　　　　　) more (　　　　　　　　) to occur in some (　　　　　　　　) (　　　　　　　　) than in America.

ヒント：be likely to do...「…する傾向にある」/ far + 比較級「はるかに〜」

(3) 次の日本語を英語にしなさい。ただし、（　）内の語（句）を順に使い、単語は必要に応じて変化させなさい。

男性主導の離婚は "talāq" と言うのに対して、女性が要求するものは "khula" と言います。前者は簡単に行われますが、後者はそうではありません。

(initiate; request; the former)

____

Chapter 7

Smile!

葬式とお見舞いの時以外は微笑まなければならない！（イタリア）

笑顔は人間関係に重要な役割を演じます。しかし、常に笑顔でいなさいと命令されたら、笑顔になりますか？微笑みの意義について掘り下げましょう。

20

Many funny laws are related to the world's most famous cities and places. Because we tend to prejudge people from other countries, we attach images to conveniently fit their nations. This is apparent when we consider a queer little law in Italy: "In Milan it is a legal requirement to smile at all times, except during funerals or hospital visits." Extensive research suggests this foolish law does not exist, so the challenge is to discover how it appeared in the first place.

Milan is the second largest city in Italy and the capital of the Lombardy region. It is a favorite destination of tourists from all over the world, due to its historical architecture, natural environment, rich cultural life and gastronomy. It is one of the most famous Italian cities after Rome.

The first reason this rumored law began circulating must be due to the way Italians are viewed by other people. They are considered "better at life," seductive, concerned about fashion and physical appearance. The famous expression, "dolce vita," or sweet life, sums up in two words the concepts defining the Italian lifestyle: passion, exquisite food, sun and hospitality. On top of this, it is commonplace for many of their cities to organize extravagantly enjoyable and colorful carnivals. Italy has a Latin culture, which is defined by a more extroverted and expansive nature than other cultures, both in the Occident and Orient. So it is no wonder that we imagine Italians wearing perpetual smiles.

Milan residents' obligation to smile all the time has two exceptions: when they take part in a funeral or when they are visiting a hospital. This little clause was probably created in order to make the "law" sound more authentic and to suggest that Italians are not insensitive people who would smile in inappropriate situations.

It is most evident that this law is a myth when running a search on it through the Web and getting no hits showing this law as real. This suggests the hypothesis above: The idea of Italians from Milan being obliged to smile all the time is a product of non-Italian peoples' imaginations. Since many have visited Milan as tourists, they must have encountered very friendly and courteous hotel and restaurant staff who smiled all the time. Moreover, when this law is mentioned as hearsay, it is common for people to say that the penalty for not smiling is a $100 fine. This can't be accurate since the currency in Italy is the Euro. This could be evidence that the rumor is from a source outside Milan and Italy.

And, after all, it is hard to imagine that one could physically be able to pull off smiling all the time. It would be exhausting and such a law, if it existed, would be abusive. And to the contrary of all this, recent survey results have indicated that Italians are in fact the unhappiest people in Europe. So, it looks like common conceptions of the collective character of various places can actually be quite wrong.

Words and Phrases

prejudge 早まった判断をする / **legal requirement** 法規定 / **the Lombardy region** ロンバルディア州 / **gastronomy** 地方独特の料理法 / **rumored** 噂になっている / **seductive** 魅力的な / **exquisite** 美味な、極上の / **extravagantly** 贅沢に / **extroverted** 外向型の / **Occident** 西洋 / **Orient** 東洋 / **perpetual** 絶え間ない / **clause** 条項 / **authentic** 信頼できる / **insensitive** 思いやりのない / **hearsay** 噂 / **pull off...** …を成し遂げる / **exhausting** 骨の折れる / **abusive** 虐待的である、[風習が]不正な

Tips

街づくりの法律

街づくりのための法律は世界各地に見られます。そのほとんどがローカルなルール、つまり条例です。アメリカのアイダホ州ポカテロ市には笑顔条例というものがあります。笑顔週間には笑顔を作らなければなりません。違反者は逮捕され、スマイルセンターで笑顔講習を受講させられるそうです。

月の土地も分譲されていますから、将来月に街ができたら、月でも笑顔を絶やしてはいけないというような法律ができるかもしれませんね。

1 VOCABULARY

次の日本語を読み、(　)に当てはまる語を選んで、英訳を完成させなさい。

(1) 外交的な生活を送るためには、笑いを義務とすることは欠かせません。
To live an (a.　　　　　　　) life, the (b.　　　　　　　) to smile is essential.

converted　delegation　extravagant　extroverted　obligation　obstruction

(2) 情熱的なホテルのスタッフなら礼儀正しい笑みを本当に売りにすることができるものです。
(a.　　　　　　　) hotel staff are able to really sell their (b.　　　　　　　) smiles.

conventional　courteous　love　passionate　perceivable　perceptual

(3) その仮説はミラノ外部の人には当てはまらず、作り話だと分かりました。
The (a.　　　　　　　) did not apply to people outside Milan and was found out to be a (b.　　　　　　　).

comeback　hypocrisy　hypotension　hypothesis　myth　prejudge

2 COMPREHENSION

A：次の問いの答えとして最も適当なものを選びなさい。

(1) According to the passage, what is the second largest city in Italy?
(A) Florence　(B) Milan　(C) Naples　(D) Rome

(2) What is NOT mentioned as one of Milan's charms?
(A) Architecture　(B) Nature　(C) Food　(D) Manufacturing

B：音声を聴きながら(　)内に単語を入れて問いを完成させ、英語で答えなさい。 21 22

(1) In what situations is there no (　　　　　　　) (　　　　　　　) Italians to (　　　　　　　) all the time?

____

(2) Why is the following (　　　　　　　) NOT (　　　　　　　)? "Italians are (　　　　　　　) $100 if they do not smile all the time."

____

3 GRAMMAR

次の(　)に当てはまる最も適当な語(句)を(A)～(D)から選びなさい。

(1) In Milan it is a legal requirement to smile at all times, (　　　　　　) not during funerals or hospital visits.

(A) and　　(B) but　　(C) or　　(D) so

(2) The first reason (　　　　　　) this rumored law began circulating must be due to the way Italians are viewed by other people.

(A) which　　(B) when　　(C) where　　(D) why

(3) It is common (　　　　　　) many of their cities to organize extravagantly enjoyable and colorful carnivals.

(A) for　　(B) of　　(C) as　　(D) that

文法のポイント

(1) 接続詞 but の用法：共通部分を省略し、強調したい部分を表現する用法がある。
(2) 関係副詞 why：the reason の後が完全文なら、why または that が後続可能。
(3) 不定詞の意味上の主語：不定詞の意味上の主語は< for+A >の形で置かれる。

4 COMPOSITION

(1) 次の日本語の意味になるように(　)内の語(句)を並べ替えなさい。

"dolce vita" という有名な表現は、イタリア人の生活様式を定義する概念を２語でまとめています。

The famous expression, "dolce vita," sums up in two words (define / the concepts / lifestyle / Italian / the / that).

____

(2) 次の日本語の意味になるように、ヒントを参考にしながら(　)を埋めなさい。

私たちは他の国の人たちについて早まった判断をしがちです。たとえば、イタリアから来た人は、みんな外向的でいつも笑っているように思います。

We are (　　　　　　) to (　　　　　　) people from other countries.
For example, we consider all the people from Italy to (　　　　　　) (　　　　　　) and always smiling.

ヒント：be apt to do...「…しがち」/ extroverted「外向性の」

(3) 次の日本語を英語にしなさい。ただし、(　)内の語(句)を順に使い、単語は必要に応じて変化させなさい。

ミラノに住むイタリア人がずっと笑顔でいないといけないという考えは、イタリア人ではない人たちの想像が生み出したものであり得ます。(idea; oblige; product)

____

Chapter 8

Silent Sunday?

午後10時以降，トイレは流してはいけない（スイス）

日曜日は誰にとっても嬉しいものです。西洋では宗教的に特別の意味を持ちます。
この章では、日曜日に騒音を禁止する法律がある国を紹介しましょう。

23

Due to their Christian legacy, most countries in Europe consider Sunday a sacred day. Traditionally, most people usually don't go to work or do any serious chores around the house. Sunday, the first day of the week for most European cultures, is dedicated to rest and relaxation. Anyone who treats Sunday as just any other day is likely to be regarded with disdain. Even worse, disturbing someone else's Sunday rest can result in being fined. This is the case in Switzerland, where some strict laws regarding Sunday are applied. In fact, these rules often cause newcomers there to feel out of place. It is important to note that the Swiss love peace and quiet as well as respecting their neighbors. Once this is understood, one can see why the Swiss treat Sunday with such reverence.

There are almost a dozen of such inane laws or practices based on social mores in Switzerland. One of the most cited rules, especially on expatriate forums, is that you are not allowed to hang clothes to dry on Sunday. There is actually no law preventing this, but most locals will frown on anyone doing this, saying it's in bad taste. Even laundry facilities are closed on Sundays with signs reminding people not to wash.

Washing a car is also discouraged and may really rattle the neighbors if done at home. According to a popular website, there are serious reasons why cars must not be washed just anywhere. A law does state that rinse water resulting from car washing must not be discharged into drains. Dirty and soapy rinse water is considered a pollutant which will affect the environment. This law seeks to prohibit polluting groundwater or rivers with water containing detergents and other chemical substances. On top of this, anyone using noisy, high pressure water cleaners is often subject to a fine.

Foreigners are also flabbergasted to learn that toilets can't be flushed after 10 PM, though there is no actual law against this. The Swiss Homeowners' Society came up with this suggestion in order to reduce wear and tear on the plumbing and to not bother neighbors. The Swiss Renter's Law, according to article 257f, states that people have the right to peace and quiet during normal sleeping hours. This implies one should take care to avoid using a toilet or shower after 10 PM. Unless neighbors agree to waive this right, it is best to comply with this law.

In addition to all of the above, noisy activities of any kind are strongly discouraged on Sundays. These include such things as dropping cans and bottles in public recycling bins, mowing the lawn, using a washing machine or hosting a party. If there must be a party, remotely located houses can be reserved for such a thing.

As peculiar as these rules may sound, and as harsh as the culture shock may be, these laws and rules reflect the quintessentially Swiss idea of respecting others' right to relax. This is exactly the reason why any kind of disturbing noise is not allowed at certain hours and on Sundays. Switzerland is recognized for its high living standards and for its pleasant environment, and after conforming to their ways of doing things, most people will enjoy their time there.

Words and Phrases

Christian legacy キリスト教が受け継いだもの / **chore** 毎日の仕事 / **dedicate** 捧げる / **disdain** 軽蔑 / **disturb** 妨げる / **reverence** 敬愛 / **inane** 馬鹿げた / **mores**（特定の社会の）しきたり / **expatriate** 国外在住の / **in bad taste** はしたない / **rattle** イライラさせる / **discharge** 排出する / **soapy** 石鹸だらけの / **pollutant** 汚染物質 / **detergent** 洗剤 / **flabbergast** 面食らわせる / **flush** トイレを水で洗い流す / **plumbing** 水道管類 / **waive**（権利などを）放棄する / **comply with**（法律などに）従う / **quintessentially** 典型的に / **disturbing noise** 雑音 / **conform to...** …に合わせる

Tips

日曜日に商取引が禁止？

日曜日は休日として、お店が開いていない国も少なくありません。敬虔なクリスチャンが多いトンガでは、日曜日は安息日として一部の例外を除き、全ての商取引が禁止されています。

フランスにおいても、日曜日はすべての労働者にとっての休日と定められています。もちろん、大都市や観光地などは例外として日曜営業が可能となっていますので、観光でフランスを訪れてもそれに気づくことはないでしょう。景気が停滞している昨今、少しでも多くの売り上げを得るため、日曜営業を実現させようとする動きもありますが、スローライフを重んじるフランスでは、お金では解決できない問題が山積しています。

1 VOCABULARY

次の日本語を読み、(　)に当てはまる語を選んで、英訳を完成させなさい。

(1) ある馬鹿げた法律により、いくつかの無害な化学物質が汚染物質であるとみなされています。
Some harmless chemical substances are classified as (a. 　　　　　　) because of an (b. 　　　　　　) law.

inane　ingrain　innate　pollutants　pollutes　pollution

(2) あなたが権利の放棄に同意したことにびっくり仰天しました。
I was (a. 　　　　　　) by the fact that you agreed to (b. 　　　　　　) the right.

flabbergasted　flamboyant　fragile　waive　wave　weave

(3) 午後 10 時以降にトイレを流してはいけないという法律を蔑んではいけません。
Don't hold the law in (a. 　　　　　　) that says "toilets can't be (b. 　　　　　　) after 10 PM."

despite　discourage　disdain　flashed　flushed　freshen

2 COMPREHENSION

A：次の問いの答えとして最も適当なものを選びなさい。

(1) Why do most countries in Europe regard Sunday as a sacred day?

(A) Requested by vote
(B) For religious reasons
(C) National policy
(D) Out of habit

(2) Why must cars NOT be washed just anywhere?

(A) Exhaust gases discharged from a running vehicle are considered pollutants.
(B) Rubbish caused by the cleaning of cars must be disposed of at home.
(C) The noise created while washing cars always disturbs neighbors.
(D) Rinse water that is a result of car washing contributes to pollution.

B：音声を聴きながら(　)内に単語を入れて問いを完成させ、英語で答えなさい。 24 25

(1) What are visitors to Switzerland (　　　　　　) to (　　　　　　) about (　　　　　　) toilets?

____

(2) Why is any (　　　　　　) of (　　　　　　) noise NOT (　　　　　　) on Sundays in Switzerland?

____

3 GRAMMAR

次の(　)に当てはまる最も適当な語(句)を(A)～(D)から選びなさい。

(1) (　　　　　　) this is understood, one can see why the Swiss treat Sunday with such reverence.

(A) What　　(B) That　　(C) Once　　(D) So

(2) Even laundry facilities are closed on Sundays, with signs (　　　　　　) people that they shouldn't wash their clothes on that day.

(A) reminding　　(B) reminded　　(C) to remind　　(D) reminds

(3) (　　　　　　) neighbors don't agree to waive this right, it is best to follow this law.

(A) What　　(B) Until　　(C) If　　(D) Unless

文法のポイント

(1) 従位接続詞：<X+完全文>が副詞節になっているなら、Xは従位接続詞。
(2) 現在分詞の形容詞用法：<X+doing... >の形。「…するX」の意味。with が前に来るとき、この with は付帯状況を表せる。
(3) 接続詞 unless：unless ~ は「～しない限り」で、if...not で置き換え可能。

4 COMPOSITION

(1) 次の日本語の意味になるように(　)内の語(句)を並べ替えなさい。

これが日曜日に、人はどんな種類の雑音も立てることが許されていない理由です。

This is (why / make / allowed / are / people / not / any / the reason / to) kind of disturbing noise on Sundays.

____

(2) 次の日本語の意味になるように、ヒントを参考にしながら(　)を埋めなさい。

スイスの人たちが隣人を尊重しているだけでなく、平和と静寂が大好きだと述べておくことは意味のあることです。

It is (　　　　　　) to note that the (　　　　　　) (　　　　　　) only respect their neighbors (　　　　　　) also love peace and (　　　　　　).

ヒント：significant「重要な、意味のある」/ quiet「静寂」

(3) 次の日本語を英語にしなさい。ただし、(　)内の語(句)を順に使い、単語は必要に応じて変化させなさい。

実際には、人が洗濯物を干すのを防ぐ法律はありませんが、その国の大半の人たちは、誰がこの行為をしても眉をひそめるでしょう。(prevent; hang; majority; frown)

____

Chapter 9

Want to Be a Pilot?

パイロットの足の長さは少なくとも90センチ？（インド）

パイロットになるには色々な条件があるものです。中には、身体的条件として身長というよりも、足の長さが重要である国もあるようです。

26

Pilots have one of the toughest jobs on the planet. It's no surprise that in order to become one, candidates must exceed certain stringent requirements. Those wishing to be pilots must undergo mental tests to gauge their mental competence and health as well as physical checks to make sure their body is fit and correctly proportioned. Failing to meet even one of the requirements may prove to be dangerous in certain situations and lead to tragic consequences. A person's physical measurements are usually taken into account in most military air forces in the world. These measurements refer to various factors, such as height, weight, height while seated, acuteness of vision, flexibility, length from buttocks to knees and so on. Because of these requirements, many silly related laws have come into effect.

One of the best known laws in this category is that regarding Indian air force pilots. It is said a pilot's legs need to measure at least 90 cm from hips to toes. No matter how tall the person is, if one has legs shorter than 90 cm, he or she will not be able to become a pilot. Rumor has it that a well-known and trustworthy lawyer, Mr. Kadambi Lakshminarasimha, stated that this rule actually exists.

People who debate the validity of this law don't need to go as far as asking an Indian lawyer to verify it for them. If we stop and consider this law for a moment, we can see it is really a serious matter. Legs have to be a certain length in order to operate the plane's pedals properly. Since these sensitive controls are used to adjust the plane's rudder as well as for braking, it is crucial the pilot be able to have full control of them at all times.

Skeptics may continue to disbelieve such a law exists. In order to clarify whether 90-cm legs are really mandatory, it is necessary to take a look at the official medical standards for officer candidates of the IAF (Indian Air Force), available on the Web. There are about 30 pages of medical and physical requirements, including even the required condition of the candidate's teeth. In these pages, one can clearly find it stated that the length of a pilot's legs must be between 99 and 120 cm. So, in truth, the rumored law that 90 cm is the cutoff between those who can qualify to be a pilot and those who can't, isn't entirely true; the parameters are actually more severe! We could say it's impossible for excessively tall people to become pilots just as it's impossible for short people to do so.

This case shows that odd laws may sometimes prove to be true and that there are serious reasons behind their adoption. Some law enthusiasts and newsmongers who get their kicks talking about strange and stupid laws may be disappointed that this Indian law is in fact not so stupid. However, that doesn't mean the topic of unusual laws is in any danger of drying up soon. Take the following interesting regulation for example: Indian military personnel cannot use swords during battle, with an exception granted to the Naga regiment. This regiment was created in 1970 and in fact their traditional weapon is the Burmese *dha*, a short sword similar to a machete. The Naga people adopted the *dha* as their own after the Burmese migrated through their region. As strange as it may seem for modern soldiers to use swords of any type in battle, this is true.

All in all, rules are no laughing matter when it comes to the military; no matter how absurd their regulations may seem for us, many are true and have a good reason for existing.

Words and Phrases

candidate 志願者 / **stringent** 厳しい / **gauge** 測定する / **height while seated** 座高 / **buttocks** 臀部 / **come into effect** 施行する / **trustworthy** 信頼できる / **validity** 合法性 / **verify** 証明する / **rudder** (飛行機の尾翼にある)方向舵 / **skeptics** 疑い深い人 / **mandatory** 必須の / **officer candidate** 幹部候補生 / **cutoff** 限界 / **enthusiast** 熱狂者 / **newsmonger** 噂話の好きな人 / **military personnel** 軍人 / **regiment** 連隊 / **Burmese** ビルマ(人、語)の / **machete** なた / **absurd** 馬鹿げた

Tips

空の細かな法律

空に対して『自由』というイメージを持っている人も多いことかと思いますが、実は空に関しては非常に細かい規定があります。建築物の高さはもちろんのこと、クレーン車の設置、樹木、アドバルーン、花火なども制限があります。規定を超える高さの建築物には航空障害灯と呼ばれる点滅式のライトを設置しなければなりません。高速ビルや鉄塔などに設置されていますので見たことがある人も多いことかと思います。

ディズニーランドでは遠近法で建物を高く見せる工夫をして高さ制限にかからないようにしているそうです。夢の国で航空障害灯が点滅していては現実に戻されてしまうという理由からだそうです。

1 VOCABULARY

次の日本語を読み、(　)に当てはまる語を選んで、英訳を完成させなさい。

(1) どんなに馬鹿げているように思えても、候補者は一定の厳しい条件を満たさなければなりません。
No matter how absurd they seem to be, (a.   ) must exceed certain (b.   ) requirements.

candidates　consumers　immigrants　string　stringent　strong

(2) 軍事ということになると、精神的能力を測定するためにメンタルテストを受けることは重要です。
When it comes to the military, it is important that recruits (a.   ) testing to (b.   ) their mental competence.

gauge　gauze　gorge　underestimate　undergo　underlie

(3) 誰であれ施行を積極的に進めることに懐疑的な目を向ける人もいますが、相当多くの馬鹿げた法律が成立しているようです。
Quite a few silly laws seem to come into (a.   ), though some people cast a (b.   ) eye on the willingness of anyone to enforce these laws.

doubting　effect　power　service　skeptical　suspected

2 COMPREHENSION

A：次の問いの答えとして最も適当なものを選びなさい。

(1) In the rumored law, what is the minimum length of a pilot's legs?

(A) 80 cm　(B) 90 cm　(C) 99 cm　(D) 120 cm

(2) Why do legs have to be a certain length to become a pilot?

(A) To be able to run fast in an emergency
(B) To promote physical strength
(C) To control the plane's pedals correctly
(D) To wear the uniforms properly

B：音声を聴きながら(　)内に単語を入れて問いを完成させ、英語で答えなさい。 27 28

(1) What is the (   ) requirement for IAF (   ) regarding the (   ) of legs?

____

(2) In what situation can Indian military (   ) use (   ) during (   )?

____

3 GRAMMAR

次の(　)に当てはまる最も適当な語(句)を(A)〜(D)から選びなさい。

(1) (　　　　　　) tall the person is, if one has legs shorter than 90 cm, he or she will not be able to become a pilot.

(A) Whoever　(B) Whenever　(C) Wherever　(D) However

(2) (　　　　　　) who debate the validity of this law don't need to go as far as asking an Indian lawyer to verify it for them.

(A) This　(B) That　(C) Those　(D) These

(3) It may be difficult for an (　　　　　　) tall man to become a pilot for the same reason that a short man has difficulty becoming one.

(A) excess　(B) excessive　(C) excessively　(D) excessiveness

文法のポイント

(1) 譲歩節を導く however：< however+形容詞 / 副詞>の形。< No matter how+形容詞 / 副詞>で置き換え可能。
(2) those who の表現：< those+who >で「〜する人々」の意味。
(3) 強意の副詞 excessively：形容詞の意味を強調する副詞。

4 COMPOSITION

(1) 次の日本語の意味になるように(　)内の語(句)を並べ替えなさい。

奇妙で馬鹿げた法律について話をするのを楽しむ噂話好きの人の中には、インドの法律がそれほど妙ではないとがっかりする人もいるかもしれません。

Some newsmongers (that / may / talking / disappointed / enjoy / be / about / laws / strange and stupid) that this Indian law isn't so stupid.

____

(2) 次の日本語の意味になるように、ヒントを参考にしながら(　)を埋めなさい。

パイロットになりたい人は、精神的能力と健康状態を測ってもらうために、メンタルテストを受けないといけません。

A person who (　　　　　　) to be a pilot must (　　　　　　) mental tests with a (　　　　　　) to (　　　　　　) his or her mental competence and health (　　　　　　).

ヒント：with a view to...「…するために」/ have...gauged「…を測ってもらう」

(3) 次の日本語を英語にしなさい。ただし、(　)内の語(句)を順に使い、単語は必要に応じて変化させなさい。

現代の兵士が戦闘中に様々なタイプの剣をも使うのは変ですが、これは事実です。

(soldiers / swords / battle / but)

____

Chapter 10

Napoleon, the Pig?

豚に「ナポレオン」の名前を付けてはならない（フランス）

ナポレオンは英雄、豚は貪欲で嫌われ者だから、豚にナポレオンの名前をつけては
ならないという法律があるという噂です。真実はどうでしょうか？

29

Napoleon Bonaparte (1769-1821) was one of the most prominent historical figures of France. He was a talented military tactician and ambitious political leader who fought many victorious battles across Europe. Napoleon is known for having himself declared Emperor of the French and for deploying a series of liberal reforms throughout Europe. From his seat of power, one of the greatest military commanders in history was able to influence civil law all over the world with his Napoleonic Code.

While he is a cultural icon to some, both past and present, popular culture has attributed to Napoleon a comical image. This was due to his short height of 170 centimeters, usually shorter than the grenadiers who may have been nearby on the battlefield, and because of his difficult personality and illusions of nobility. Whether to protect his image or to slander him, there is a famous rumor saying that you can't name your pig "Napoleon" in France. But is it true?

Before looking for other evidence, it needs to be mentioned that there exists a literary reference which has probably contributed to the myth that it is illegal to name a pig "Napoleon." George Orwell's dystopian and allegorical novel *Animal Farm* from 1945 features a character named Napoleon, who is in fact a pig. This boar is the main antagonist of *Animal Farm*, and is in fact a satirical version of Stalin. In the first French version of the novel, this character was named Cesar. This seeming sensitivity has possibly led to people thinking that there is actually a law regarding French livestock names.

With all this in mind, it becomes a bit easier to understand the reason why this rumor is considered to be true. It needs to be mentioned, once and for all, that there is no law preventing you from calling a pig "Napoleon" in France. Historians interested in researching myths have checked the French Civil Code and other laws from the mid-19th century on and there is no trace of such a law. As for today's regulations, there is also no evidence of a law interfering with a person's preference for naming animals after famous figures.

On the other hand, there are several other reasons why this rumor has gained credibility. In spite of Napoleon Bonaparte's fame in Western civilization, his image has always juxtaposed a clownish imp who is also a calculating and astute conqueror, full of narcissistic pomp. Historically, he was a contradictory character, ruthless and with a volcanic temper, yet able to display copious amounts of affection towards people at the same time. British print propaganda at the time depicted him in caricature as a man of extremely short stature, though his height was actually relatively average for men at the time. This led to the idea of the Napoleon complex. It is considered that men of short stature sometimes display aggressive social behavior in order to compensate for being "vertically challenged." It's no wonder that people started to imagine that Napoleon had taken some measures in order to prevent others from mocking him, including ridiculous ideas like the "law" in question. More than this, the French are known for being patriotic and regarding their national symbols with pride, which makes this myth plausible, even if it is not confirmed.

In the end, it looks like you can go to France, raise a pig and name it Napoleon without any worry. So, this law remains just another funny fact that puts smiles on people's faces when they read about French culture.

Words and Phrases

tactician 策士 / **victorious battles** 征服戦争 / **deploy** 配備する / **seat of power** 権力の座 / **cultural icon** 文化の象徴 / **grenadier** 手榴弾兵 / **nobility** 高貴な生まれ / **slander** 中傷する / **dystopian** 悲惨な / **allegorical** 寓話から成る / **boar** 雄ブタ / **antagonist** 敵対者 / **a satirical version of...** …の皮肉版 / **juxtapose** 並列する / **clownish** 滑稽な / **imp** いたずらっ子 / **astute** 抜け目のない / **narcissistic** 自己陶酔的な / **pomp** 尊大さ / **ruthless** 無慈悲な / **volcanic temper** 激しい気性 / **copious** 豊富な / **mock** 馬鹿にする

Tips

動物に関する法律

動物に関する法律は世界各地に見られます。デンマークやオーストラリアは動物愛護先進国と言ってもよいでしょう。デンマークでは豚舎で豚が自由に動き回れるように指定した法律があります。豚舎にエアコンを入れたりするほど豚にストレスを与えないように愛護を徹底しています。

一方で、ある国の動物園では殺処分のキリンを一般公開にて解体し、ライオンの餌にしたことで愛護活動家などから非難を受けています。

1 VOCABULARY

次の日本語を読み、（　）に当てはまる語(句)を選んで、英訳を完成させなさい。

(1) 家畜に有名人の名前を付けることは民法で禁じられています。
Naming (a. 　　　　　　) after famous figures is prohibited by (b. 　　　　　　) law.

civil　constitution　criminal　householders　livestock　stockbreeders

(2) 現行の法律では、歴史上有名な人物をあざけることは違法です。
(a. 　　　　　　) to current laws, (b. 　　　　　　) prominent historical figures is illegal.

according　as　make fun of　mocking　related　ridicule

(3) 政権の主たる敵対者は、風刺画で指導者を醜い野獣として描写しました。
The main (a. 　　　　　　) of the regime depicted the leader in (b. 　　　　　　) as a deformed brute.

antagonism　antagonist　caricature　cartoonist　contradiction　photocopy

2 COMPREHENSION

A：次の問いの答えとして最も適当なものを選びなさい。

(1) In the first French version of *Animal Farm*, what was the porcine character's name?
(A) George　(B) Napoleon　(C) Stalin　(D) Cesar

(2) Why do short men sometimes display aggressive social behavior?
(A) To make up for being short　(B) To overcome their mental weakness
(C) To show their strong points　(D) To make up with their enemies

B：音声を聴きながら（　）内に単語を入れて問いを完成させ、英語で答えなさい。　30 31

(1) What does "(　　　　　　) challenged", (　　　　　　) 17 (　　　　　　) page 43, (　　　　　　)?

____

(2) Why does Napoleon have a (　　　　　　) (　　　　　　) in (　　　　　　) culture?

____

3 GRAMMAR

次の(　)に当てはまる最も適当な語(句)を(A)～(D)から選びなさい。

(1) There (　　　　　　　) a literary reference which has probably contributed to the myth that it is illegal to name a pig "Napoleon."

(A) lie　　(B) lies　　(C) lain　　(D) lying

(2) There is no law keeping you (　　　　　　　) a pig "Napoleon" in France.

(A) to call　　(B) are calling　　(C) from calling　　(D) called

(3) Napoleon was known for (　　　　　　　) a series of reforms throughout Europe.

(A) effect　　(B) to effect　　(C) effecting　　(D) effected

文法のポイント

(1) be 動詞以外の there 構文：there の直後に live, stand, exist, lie, appear, occur, grow, come, arise などの動詞（存在や出現の動詞）を用いることが可能。
(2) keep の語法：< keep+O+from doing >の形は「O に～させない」の意味。
(3) 前置詞のあとの準動詞：前置詞のあとは名詞性の強い動名詞が来る。

4 COMPOSITION

(1) 次の日本語の意味になるように(　)内の語(句)を並べ替えなさい。
ナポレオンはフランス皇帝であると自ら宣言したことで知られています。
Napoleon (is / having / declared / himself / for / known) Emperor of the French.

____

(2) 次の日本語の意味になるように、ヒントを参考にしながら(　)を埋めなさい。
イギリスの出版業界の宣伝で、ナポレオンは身長の低い人物として風刺されて描かれました。しかし、ナポレオンの身長は平均的な高さでした。
British print propaganda (　　　　　　　) Napoleon in caricature as a man (　　　　　　　) short (　　　　　　　). Notwithstanding, he had an (　　　　　　　) (　　　　　　　).

ヒント：short stature「低身長」/ average「平均的な、普通の」

(3) 次の日本語を英語にしなさい。ただし、(　)内の語(句)を順に使い、単語は必要に応じて変化させなさい。
有名人にちなんで動物に名前をつけるという個人的な楽しみを奪う法律が存在してよい根拠はどこにもありません。
(no reason; deprive A of B; name A after B)

____

Chapter 11

Don't Drop Dead Here!

国会議事堂内で死んではいけない？（イギリス）

死んではいけない場所があるようです。たとえば、宮殿内で倒れてはいけません。
国葬にしないといけないからだそうです。本当のところはどうなのでしょう。

32

Almost every country in the world has its own set of outlandish laws. There are many such laws in the United Kingdom. Placing a postage stamp depicting the British monarch upside down is considered an act of treason. In Scotland, one is obliged to let in anyone who comes to the door and asks to use the toilet. A survey asking participants what they thought the dumbest laws were was taken a few years ago, and its results were published by *The Telegraph* and other newspapers. According to the results, the law deeming it illegal to die in the Houses of Parliament was chosen by 27% of the 3,931 voters.

The prohibition of dying in certain places is a social and political phenomenon which occurs in other countries as well. Prohibition of death first appeared in human history on the Greek island of Delos, where it was enacted for religious reasons. Nowadays, there are some towns in France and in Spain that people are not allowed to die in because of a lack of cemetery plots. In the Norwegian town of Longyearbyen, death is prohibited because the buried bodies don't decompose due to the low temperature of the permafrost soil in this Arctic region. Though these laws seem a bit far-fetched, there are still new attempts to pass laws outlawing death. For instance, the mayor of the Brazilian town of Biritiba Mirim unsuccessfully tried to introduce such a law in 2005 because the local cemetery had reached full capacity.

Taking these cases into consideration, it may seem like the interdiction of a person dying in the Houses of Parliament could be true. In fact, this is a myth. This law came about as a consequence of another myth, which states that anyone who dies in Westminster Palace will receive an extravagant state funeral. Since state funerals are organized only for monarchs, any commoner who is about to die must be immediately removed from the premises of Westminster. Being entitled to a state funeral if you die in the Houses of Parliament may have been true centuries ago. In order to lessen the chances of any deaths occurring in the Palace, a law was passed in 1279 that banned people from wearing armor there. Without armor-clad weapon-bearing folk hanging around Parliament, there was less of a chance of violent fighting and deaths. Many such laws were applied in the past, according to books like *The Strange Laws of Old England* by Nigel Cawthorne.

An article on a BBC site about weird laws in Britain informed that laws seeking to prohibit deaths in Parliament or guarantee state funerals for those who die there do not exist. A spokesman from the House of Commons apparently confirmed this as nothing but rumor. Anyone who dies in Westminster will be under the jurisdiction of the coroner of the Royal Household, but will not be entitled to a state funeral. Indeed, there have been past cases of people dying at Westminster and none benefited from a state funeral.

Words and Phrases

outlandish 風変わりな / **postage stamp** 郵便切手 / **monarch** 専制君主 / **an act of treason** 謀反 / **the Houses of Parliament** 国会議事堂 / **cemetery plots** 墓地の区画 / **Norwegian** ノルウェーの / **decompose** 腐敗する / **permafrost** 永久凍土層 / **far-fetched** こじつけの / **outlaw** 禁止する / **interdiction** 禁止 / **extravagant** 非常に豪華な / **commoner** 一般人 / **the premises of...** …の屋敷・構内 / **lessen the chances** 可能性を減らす / **armor-clad** 鎧を着た / **weapon-bearing** 武装した / **jurisdiction** 管轄 / **coroner** 検死官

Tips

死に方に関する法律

死に関する法律や条例は少なくありません。日本では火葬していますが、宗教上の理由などから土葬の地域もあります。土葬は火葬に比べ大きな土地が必要となります。そのため、都市化が進行している地域では、土地不足が深刻な問題となっています。

埋葬用地不足を解消するための苦肉の策として『死ぬことを禁じる』などという法案が出てくるかもしれません。近年はペットの埋葬なども問題となっているようです。一方で、『死ぬ権利』が議論されていることも頭の片隅に置かなければなりません。

1 VOCABULARY

次の日本語を読み、(　)に当てはまる語を選んで、英訳を完成させなさい。

(1) イギリスの風変りな法律の 1 つに、国王の切手を上下さかさまに添付すると反逆罪とみなされるというものがあります。
An outlandish law in the U.K. states that placing a postage stamp depicting the British monarch (a.　　　　　) is regarded as an act of (b.　　　　　).

downside up　　inside out　　treason　　treasure　　treaty　　upside down

(2) 墓地不足を低減するため、ある都市内での死を禁じることは効果的でしょう。
In order to (a.　　　　　) the shortage of cemeteries, the (b.　　　　　) of dying in some cities may be effective.

bar　　bottom　　inhibition　　lessen　　low　　prohibition

(3) 国家に貢献した者は、死後、非常に高価な国葬を受ける権利が与えられます。
People who have contributed significantly to the country are (a.　　　　　) to have an (b.　　　　　) national funeral when they die.

ample　　entire　　entitled　　extravagant　　illegal　　honored

2 COMPREHENSION

A：次の問いの答えとして最も適当なものを選びなさい。

(1) What country's people should welcome another person when he or she asks to use their house's toilet?
(A) England　　(B) Scotland　　(C) France　　(D) Spain

(2) Why did the mayor of a Brazilian town try to introduce the law in question in 2005?
(A) The cemetery was fully occupied.　　(B) The cemetery was vacant.
(C) The previous law expired.　　(D) He didn't want people to die in his town.

B：音声を聴きながら(　)内に単語を入れて問いを完成させ、英語で答えなさい。 33 34

(1) In what way is sticking a (　　　　　) stamp (　　　　　) a picture of the British (　　　　　) on an envelope considered an act of (　　　　　)?

____

(2) Why must a person who is (　　　　　) quickly be (　　　　　) from the (　　　　　) of Westminster?

____

3 GRAMMAR

次の(　)に当てはまる最も適当な語(句)を(A)～(D)から選びなさい。

(1) In Scotland, one is obliged to let in (　　　　　　　) comes to the door and asks to use the toilet.

(A) whoever　(B) whomever　(C) whenever　(D) wherever

(2) There are some towns in France and Spain that people are not allowed to die in (　　　　　　　) a lack of cemetery plots.

(A) because　(B) owing to　(C) on account　(D) instead

(3) There have been past cases of (　　　　　　　) at Westminster and none received state funerals.

(A) people's dead　(B) people die　(C) people dying　(D) people died

文法のポイント

(1) 複合関係代名詞 whoever：＜ anyone+who ＞ (=anyone that) の意味。
(2) 理由を表す文と句：後続するのが文なら because, since, as が、句なら because of, due to, owing to, on account of, by reason of などが来る。
(3) 動名詞の意味上の主語：＜名詞(N) of X doing... ＞の形で、「X が…する N」の意味の場合、X は動名詞の意味上の主語となる。

4 COMPOSITION

(1) **次の日本語の意味になるように(　)内の語(句)を並べ替えなさい。**

人々が鎧をまとうことを禁じた法律が 1279 年に通過しました。

The law (which / banned / wearing / people / from / armor) was passed in 1279.

____

(2) **次の日本語の意味になるように、ヒントを参考にしながら(　)を埋めなさい。**

そこに出席した人々に、最も馬鹿げている法律は何であると彼らが思っているかを尋ねる調査が数年前に実施されました。

A survey asking the participants there (　　　　　) (　　　　　) (　　　　　) the dumbest laws (　　　　　) was (　　　　　) a few years ago.

ヒント：what S V S' be は、「S' が何であると S が V するのか」(SV は挿入節)

(3) **次の日本語を英語にしなさい。ただし、(　)内の語(句)を順に使い、単語は必要に応じて変化させなさい。**

イギリスの奇妙な法律に関する BBC のウェブサイト記事によれば、国会議事堂で死んだ人のための国葬を約束することを求めた法律は存在しないと言います。

(seek; guarantee; state funeral; the Houses of Parliament)

____

Chapter 12

Cheating Does Not Pay

カンニングをしたら刑務所行き？（バングラデッシュ）

試験中にカンニングをしてはいけないですね。日本の大学では単位をたくさん落とすことになるでしょう。でも、世界には投獄されるところもあるようです。

35

Cheating in school is never encouraged or well regarded in any country in the world. A person who cheats is using the hard work of others in order to gain an advantage without showing any real effort themselves. On top of this, it is impossible to accurately evaluate a cheater's true abilities. It is for these reasons that cheating is usually discouraged. In some cultures, this negative behavior is unfortunately tolerated, while in other countries, cheating is harshly reprimanded. Things become more serious when it comes to final exams, because the grade that the candidate is awarded has a significant impact on his or her future. In most cases, if someone is caught cheating during important exams, he or she will most likely be expelled from the examination room and probably not be given the chance to retake the exam.

In some countries, the consequences of cheating are no laughing matter. Bangladeshi children aged 15 and over can allegedly be sent to jail if they cheat during final examinations. This potential penalty for cheating is well known throughout Bangladesh as students are reminded through extensive media campaigns. Though it is common knowledge there that a person can be imprisoned for cheating, there is a question as to the origins of this law and how much legal precedent it has.

Bangladesh is a country in South Asia bordered by India along its borders in the north, east and west. As its neighbor with a shared history, India has had an overwhelming influence on Bangladeshi culture. This has caused the country to adopt the principles of the Indian Penal Code. Bangladesh was part of Pakistan, which, in turn, was part of India under British governance. This British-influenced code, in Chapter XVII, provides certain regulations regarding cheating, but not necessarily regarding exams (sections 415 to 420).

On the other hand, there is relatively scant evidence of children actually spending time in jail in Bangladesh for cheating on tests. A much more important issue is the fact that many Bangladeshi children are forced to work in factories instead of having the chance to play and study. It is estimated that almost 5 million children of ages between 5 and 15 are laborers, many working without pay.

So the Bangladeshi government's threat of sending children to jail for cheating may prove to be an empty one. Either way, it is hard to believe that a child could officially be sent to jail for cheating during exams. What is true is that students who have been expelled from exams because of cheating have sporadically organized protests over the last few years.

There are some countries where a cheater can indeed go to jail if they are found guilty of misconduct during final exams. In West African countries such as Nigeria, a person can be fined or subject to incarceration for up to five years if caught illegally tampering with official forms or testing materials. This law also takes into account those with an intent to cheat.

As long as they are not abusive, measures taken in order to prevent children and students from cheating on exams are welcome and necessary. In fact, it would be unfair to trivialize the efforts of those students who have worked hard in order to pass exams with high grades. It is important to teach children the importance of being honest from the earliest stages of life, but without violating their rights.

Words and Phrases

cheating カンニング / **well regarded** 評判の良い / **on top of...** …に加えて / **cheater** カンニングをする人 / **tolerate** 許容する / **harshly** 厳しく / **reprimand** 叱責する / **expel** 追い出す / **no laughing matter** 笑い事でない / **Bangladeshi** バングラデッシュの / **allegedly** 伝えられるところでは / **imprison** 投獄する / **legal precedent** 判例 / **overwhelming** 圧倒的な / **Indian Penal Code** インド刑法 / **British governance** 英国による統治 / **scant evidence** 僅かな証拠 / **sporadically** 散発的に / **misconduct** 不正行為 / **incarceration** 投獄 / **tamper with...** …を許可なく改ざんする / **trivialize...** …をつまらないものにする（甲斐のないものにする）

Tips

喧嘩両成敗の法律

信賞必罰（しんしょうひつばつ）という考え方は程度の差こそあれ、どの国にもあるようです。法律のほとんどが罰則を制定したものであり、どちらか一方に軍配を上げるものが多いと言えます。しかしながら、中には喧嘩両成敗という法律もあります。

わが国が誇る funny laws の 1 つは『決闘罪』です。明治 22 年制定の古い法律ですが、平成 17 年の検察の統計では 34 名がこの罪名で受理されています。決闘を申し込んだ方は決闘罪、それに応じた方は決闘挑応罪となります。他にも決闘立会罪、決闘場所提供罪などが定められています。

1 VOCABULARY

次の日本語を読み、(　)に当てはまる語(句)を選んで、英訳を完成させなさい。

(1) 学生にカンニングを思いとどまらせる方法はいくつかあります。
There are some ways to (a. 　　　　　　) students from (b. 　　　　　　).

beating　cheating　cunning　discourage　remind　unthinking

(2) 公平を目的とし、その判例が以前に確立していました。
To be fair, a (a. 　　　　　　) was previously (b. 　　　　　　).

constructed	established	expelled
legal antecedent	legal loophole	legal precedent

(3) 誰かを叱責する際には、その人の権利を侵害していないか確認しなければなりません。
When you (a. 　　　　　　) someone, you must make sure that you are not (b. 　　　　　　) his/her rights.

angry　broken　cheating　reprimand　upset　violating

2 COMPREHENSION

A：次の問いの答えとして最も適当なものを選びなさい。

(1) How old are Bangladeshi children who are sent to jail if they cheat during final examinations?

(A) Between 5 and 15　(B) Older than 15 years of age
(C) Age 15 or younger　(D) Age 15 and over

(2) What was Pakistan a part of in the past?

(A) Bangladesh　(B) India　(C) England　(D) British Isles

B：音声を聴きながら(　)内に単語を入れて問いを完成させ、英語で答えなさい。 36 37

(1) Why is the act of children (　　　　　　) (　　　　　　) final (　　　　　　) (　　　　　　) so seriously?

____

(2) What is probably (　　　　　　) more important than the (　　　　　　) of cheating on (　　　　　　) in Bangladesh?

____

3 GRAMMAR

次の(　)に当てはまる最も適当な語(句)を(A)～(D)から選びなさい。

(1) Cheating is an act of using the efforts of others without permission; it is (　　　　　　) that cheating is usually discouraged.

(A) this reason　(B) for this reason　(C) to reason　(D) reasoning this

(2) There are some countries (　　　　　　) a cheater can indeed go to jail if he or she is found guilty of misconduct during final exams.

(A) in that　(B) in which　(C) of that　(D) of whom

(3) It is common knowledge there that a person can be imprisoned for cheating; however, there is a question as to the origins of this law and (　　　　　　).

(A) how many legal precedents have them
(B) how many legal precedents they have
(C) how much legal precedent does it have
(D) how much legal precedent it has

文法のポイント

(1) 強調構文：< it is X that... >の形。X は名詞、副詞、前置詞句。X に形容詞と動詞は来ない。
(2) 前置詞＋関係代名詞：完全文が後続。関係代名詞の that はこの構造では不可。
(3) 間接疑問文：直接疑問文と異なり、SV は平叙文の語順。

4 COMPOSITION

(1) 次の日本語の意味になるように(　)内の語(句)を並べ替えなさい。

実際のことだが、カンニングが原因で試験を追い出された生徒が抗議集会をしたことが過去に何度かあります。

What is true (who / that / students / have / expelled / from exams / been / is) because of cheating have organized protests several times.

____

(2) 次の日本語の意味になるように、ヒントを参考にしながら(　)を埋めなさい。

カンニングをした人の本当の能力は、正確に評価するのは不可能です。

A cheater's (　　　　　　) abilities (　　　　　　) (　　　　　　) to (　　　　　　) accurately.

ヒント：O is 難易・快不快・不可能形容詞 to V.「O は V するのが～だ」

(3) 次の日本語を英語にしなさい。ただし、(　)内の語(句)を順に使い、単語は必要に応じて変化させなさい。

子供たちに、人生の早い段階から正直であることの重要性を教えることはとても大切ですが、彼らの権利を侵害することはあってはなりません。(vital; stage; violate)

____

Chapter 13

Putting a Stop to Traffic Jams

排気ガスが多い車は市街地走行禁止（スウェーデン）

車が増える現代、どこの国でも大都市では交通渋滞が悩みの種です。そこで、この問題を回避する対策のため、不思議な法律が幾つか生まれています。

38

For most people, cars are one of the most convenient means of transportation. The accessibility of cars from the 20th century on has irreversibly changed the world we live in. There is no doubt that cars have granted us increased mobility, comfort and greater efficiency; however, this invention hasn't been without its share of drawbacks. Now that cars are so prevalent, traffic has become more congested and pollution levels are threatening our health and environment. Some countries have considered a series of measures or suggestions to encourage people to use their cars less often.

In some places, severe restrictions have been introduced. One such edict limits the amount of cars on certain days of the week based on their license plate numbers. This may seem heavy-handed and even a bit of an exaggeration, but in fact it is true. There are certain locations around the world where this law is on the books, though it hasn't always had positive results.

The rationing of road space is applied during peak periods in certain crowded areas such as city centers. This strategy is used by a number of countries, especially in Latin America. Driving on certain days has been subject to restrictions based on license plate numbers in Athens (since 1982), Santiago, Chile (1986), Mexico City (1989), Sao Paulo (1997), Bogota, Colombia (1998), La Paz, Bolivia (2003), the entirety of Honduras (2008) and in Quito, Ecuador (2010).

Such measures were also taken in Beijing in 2008 during the Summer Olympics. In the past, other communist countries have resorted to this as well. On Sundays in communist Romania, cars with license plates featuring even numbers were allowed, and on the following Sunday, cars with odd numbered plates took to the road. There had been an attempt in Paris to implement this type of law in March 2014; however, the effort failed.

Low emission zones like those implemented by Stockholm since 1996 ban cars with high emissions from certain areas of the city, thus offering drivers one more reason to upgrade their cars. This is one of the few truly successful traffic restriction measures in the world.

So while some of these laws have helped matters, experts say that drivers' ploys to bypass some of the laws actually have a more negative impact than if there had been no law at all. Among the schemes drivers use to skirt the law, having two cars instead of one, with opposing number plates, ends up doing the most damage. In order to afford two cars, car owners buy cheaper, less fuel-efficient vehicles which result in an increase of CO_2 levels. Some researchers argue that authorities should instead focus on encouraging drivers to use particle filters and to invest in cleaner cars.

There is another unfortunate aspect to these restrictions: Prohibiting drivers from using their cars causes discontent and disruption. This fact doesn't seem to matter so much, though, for legislators whose aim is to get as many vehicles off the road as possible.

In conclusion, it looks like such measures are usually ineffective in developing countries, where drivers tend to buy a second, less fuel-efficient car. The debate around road space rationing shows that preventative laws which attack the symptom and not the cause fall short of their intended goal. And naturally, people are not happy with laws that hamper their quality of life by lessening their freedom to get around. The implementation of complex proactive strategies would most likely be of greater benefit. These could include encouraging people to use alternative means of transportation by ensuring a convenient infrastructure exists for walking, cycling and access to public transportation.

Words and Phrases

irreversibly 後戻りできないほどに / **drawback** 故障 / **prevalent** 普及している / **heavy-handed** 荒っぽい / **on the books** 記録されて / **ration** ～の支給(提供)を制限する / **resort to...** …に頼る / **take to the road** 道を走れる / **implement** 実行する / **ploy** 策略 / **bypass** 出し抜く / **scheme** 悪だくみ / **skirt** 避ける / **discontent** 不満 / **disruption** 混乱 / **preventative** 予防の（=preventive）/ **fall short of**（目標に）達しない / **proactive** 先を見越した

Tips

法律の条文は古めかしい！

法律の条文というものは古めかしく、読むのも嫌だと言う人もいることでしょう。時代の流れを反映しない古い法律は多数存在します。車が登場する前は馬や馬車を使っていたわけですから、長い間改正されていない法律であれば『馬車』を『自動車』に置き換えることなく、そのまま残っています。

現代は車社会と言われていますが、小型ジェットなど、空の交通手段が一般化すれば、空にも地上のような交通ルールが適用されるかもしれません。そうなったとき、『いまどき車の法律なんて』と笑い話のネタになってしまうかもしれません。

1 VOCABULARY

次の日本語を読み、（　）に当てはまる語を選んで、英訳を完成させなさい。

(1) 最も便利な交通手段は車と言っても過言ではありません。
It is no (a.) to say that the most convenient (b.) of transportation is a car.

exaggeration　exhibition　extraction　mean　meaning　means

(2) その法を回避するため、住民は奇数のナンバープレートを付けた車と偶数のナンバープレートを付けた車の両方を所有しています。
To (a.) the law, residents own both a car with (b.) number license plates and a car with even number license plates.

enforce　jacket　odd　skirt　strange　whole

(3) 違法駐車がスムーズな交通の妨げとなり、結局、渋滞となってしまいます。
Illegal parking (a.) smooth traffic and (b.) up contributing to traffic jams.

bumpers　ceases　ends　finishes　hampers　pumps

2 COMPREHENSION

A： 次の問いの答えとして最も適当なものを選びなさい。

(1) Why do car owners buy cheaper, less fuel-efficient vehicles?

(A) To not bypass some of the laws
(B) To be able to easily own two cars
(C) To get eco-friendly cars
(D) To wait for a better car

(2) What do low emission zones like those implemented by Stockholm since 1996 prohibit people from using in certain areas of the city?

(A) All vehicles including cars, buses and trucks
(B) Vehicles with upgraded functions
(C) Cars that emit a lot of exhaust fumes
(D) Large-sized cars and buses with high emissions

B： 音声を聴きながら（　）内に単語を入れて問いを完成させ、英語で答えなさい。 39 40

(1) In what part of the world is the ( ) of ( ) road ( ) ( ) used?

____

(2) How were the ( ) on cars ( ) ( ) Sundays in ( )?

____

3 GRAMMAR

次の(　)に当てはまる最も適当な語(句)を(A)～(D)から選びなさい。

(1) (　　　　　　　) cars are so prevalent, traffic jams are common and pollution levels are threatening our health and environment.

(A) As for　　(B) Now that　　(C) So that　　(D) Except that

(2) There are certain locations around the world where this law is on the books; (　　　　　　　), it hasn't always had positive results.

(A) however　　(B) otherwise　　(C) but　　(D) though

(3) There had been an attempt in Paris to implement this type of law in March 2014, (　　　　　　　) the effort failed.

(A) owing to　　(B) instead of　　(C) but　　(D) however

文法のポイント

(1) A + that の表現：A に so, now, in, except 等が来る接続表現に注意する。
(2) 逆接の接続表現：等位接続詞（but）、従位接続詞（though）、接続副詞（however）。
(3) 前置詞と接続詞の後続要素：原則として、前置詞の後は名詞句、接続詞の後には節<主語＋動詞>が来る。

4 COMPOSITION

(1) 次の日本語の意味になるように(　)内の語(句)を並べ替えなさい。

20 世紀以降、車が利用できるようになったので、我々 1 人ひとりの住む世界は後戻りできないほど変化しました。

The accessibility of cars from the 20th century on (lives in / every / changed / has / the world / one of / irreversibly / us).

____

(2) 次の日本語の意味になるように、ヒントを参考にしながら(　)を埋めなさい。

専門家によれば、法律の幾つかを避けようとするドライバーの悪だくみは、法律が全く存在しなかった場合よりもマイナスの影響があります。

(　　　　　　　) say that drivers' (　　　　　　　) to (　　　　　　　) some of the laws have a more (　　　　　　　) (　　　　　　　) than if (　　　　　　　) (　　　　　　　) been no law at all.

ヒント：scheme「悪だくみ」/ skirt「避ける」/ negative「マイナスの」

(3) 次の日本語を英語にしなさい。ただし、(　)内の語(句)を順に使い、単語は必要に応じて変化させなさい。

できるだけ道路から多くの乗り物を排除する目的を持つ立法者にとって、ドライバーの不満はそれほど重要でないようです。(legislator; aim; discontent; matter)

____

Chapter 14

The Laws of the Jungle

カンガルーにビールを６杯以上飲ませてはいけない（オーストラリア）

この章では動物に関わる妙な法律を紹介します。動物虐待にならないことと、
動物が人に危害を加えないようにするという両面が必要なようです。

41

Dumb laws are usually just humorous rumors which, when put under the microscope, are shown to be nothing but myths. Many of these laws are said to exist in order to prevent unusual behavior with animals. It is these types of rumored rules that are most fun to examine. One of the most famous such laws is, "It is illegal to force a kangaroo to drink more than 6 bottles of beer." This wacky law is popularly referred to on the Web; however, there is no evidence that this law is real. The mechanisms behind the emergence of these types of foolish laws involving animals are worth investigating.

Some of these inane laws are completely fictional, while others originate from truths which have been misinterpreted. For instance, "Dogs may not bark after 6 PM" sounds absolutely ridiculous and there is no way a dog owner can prevent their pet from barking without resorting to animal cruelty. Taking a moment to consider the origins of this law can lead to an understanding of just how this idea came to be. A dog owner can be charged with disturbing the peace if their noisy dog can't be controlled (or simply put in the house) and its barking bothers neighbors so much that they decide to press charges. So it turns out the fictional law is based on the fact that noisiness at night can result in a fine, except it has been taken slightly out of context.

There are two reasons why the rumor of ordinance regarding kangaroos and beer came to be. First of all, the kangaroo is a national symbol of Australia. When thinking about Australia, the image of the kangaroo quickly comes to most people's minds. On the other hand, there are many stories revolving around drinking 6 cans of beer a day. Some say 6 cans of beer is healthy for the heart, while others say consuming 6 cans a day contributes to liver disease. Other recommendations state that you should not drink more than 6 cans of beer in a single sitting, but all these facts are inaccurate. It is possible for the two concepts, the kangaroo and the 6 cans of beer, to have amalgamated and to have caused the emergence of this funny law.

This is not the only dopey law regarding animals in Australia. People also get a good laugh when they hear that it is against the law to throw a bag containing both dogs and cats together into the Parramatta River. However, it is permissible to throw a bag of only dogs or only cats into the water. Another funny law about animals in Australia says that "People may not come within 100 meters of a dead whale carcass." Once again, we don't know for sure if this is true, but it is surely not a smart idea to get too close to a whale's rotting body. Not only is it extremely unpleasant, but decomposing whales may explode because of gas building up inside the remains. Avoiding danger due to any sharks eating the carrion may also be a reason behind this law.

Like most silly laws regarding animals, "It is illegal to force a kangaroo to drink more than 6 bottles of beer" seems highly implausible, but may have some basis in reality.

Words and Phrases

put A under the microscope Aを詳細に調べる / **wacky** 風変わりな / **inane** 馬鹿げた / **animal cruelty** 動物虐待 / **press charges** 告発する / **inaccurate** 不正確な / **amalgamate** 結びつく / **dopey** 愚かな / **the Parramatta River** パラマタ川(シドニー郊外のパラマタを流れる川) / **permissible** 許される / **carcass** 死骸 / **rot** 腐る / **decomposing** 腐敗している / **remains** 死体、なきがら / **carrion** 腐肉 / **implausible** あり得ない

Tips

ペットと法律

ペットの飼い主には大きな責任がつきまといます。しかしながら、「かわいい」が先行し、その責任を認識している人が少ないように思います。放し飼いにした犬が人を襲う事例は少なくありません。イギリスでも先日、犬が人を襲った場合の罰則を強化したばかりです。

また、飼育放棄も大きな問題となっています。平成24年度の犬猫を合わせた引取り数は209,388匹（内、殺処分数は161,867匹）。減少傾向にはありますが、いまだ飼育放棄をする人が多いと指摘されています。東京都動物の愛護及び管理に関する条例第5条では『動物の所有者は、動物をその終生にわたり飼養するよう努めなければならない』等、飼い主として当然すべきことをあえて条文化しています。

1 VOCABULARY

次の日本語を読み、（　）に当てはまる語を選んで、英訳を完成させなさい。

(1) 動物虐待という手段に訴えることなく犬をしつけることは、時々困難であり得ます。
Training a dog without (a. 　　　　　) to animal (b. 　　　　　) can sometimes be difficult.

crucial　cruel　cruelty　repeating　reporting　resorting

(2) 彼はその奇抜な法律に対する理解が不正確なため、隣人は迷惑していました。
Due to his (a. 　　　　　) understanding of the unusual law, his neighbor was (b. 　　　　　).

annoying　bothered　inaccurate　inappropriate　incorporate　troublesome

(3) 法律によって海面に現れたいかなる死体にも、近づくことは許されません。
By law, it is not (a. 　　　　　) to approach any animal remains that have (b. 　　　　　) from the sea.

emerged　immersed　imminent　impermissible　permissible　permissive

2 COMPREHENSION

A：次の問いの答えとして最も適当なものを選びなさい。

(1) Where can we find the funny law: "It is illegal to force a kangaroo to drink more than 6 bottles of beer?"

(A) In a law report　(B) In the library　(C) On TV　(D) On the Internet

(2) What is NOT the reason behind the law that states people may not come within 100 meters of a whale carcass?

(A) It may cause extreme discomfort to be too close to the rotting body.
(B) Decomposing whales may explode due to gas accumulating inside the carcass.
(C) People may be attacked by sharks that are eating the remains.
(D) Any person who is found standing by the whale may be accused of killing it.

B：音声を聴きながら（　）内に単語を入れて問いを完成させ、英語で答えなさい。 42 43

(1) Why is the kangaroo the (　　　　　) of a (　　　　　) (　　　　　) in (　　　　　)?

____

(2) What (　　　　　) of (　　　　　) should people NOT (　　　　　) (　　　　　) the Parramatta River?

____

3 GRAMMAR

次の(　)に当てはまる最も適当な語(句)を(A)〜(D)から選びなさい。

(1) Many of these laws are said to exist (　　　　　　) preventing unusual behavior with animals.

(A) in order to　(B) with a view to　(C) so that　(D) so as not to

(2) The mechanisms behind the emergence of these types of foolish laws involving animals are worth (　　　　　　).

(A) to investigate　(B) investigating　(C) of investigating　(D) to be investigated

(3) It turns out the fictional law is based on the fact that noisiness at night can (　　　　　　) a fine, except it has been taken slightly out of context.

(A) follow　(B) be following by　(C) be followed　(D) be followed by

文法のポイント

(1) 目的を表す表現：in order to や so as to の直後には原形不定詞、for the purpose of や with a view to の直後には動名詞、so that の直後には節が来る。
(2) 能動受動態：<worth/need/deserve＋動名詞>は能動態で受動態の意味を表す。
(3) follow の語法：A follows B は B precedes A と同意で、A が後で B が先。

4 COMPOSITION

(1) **次の日本語の意味になるように(　)内の語(句)を並べ替えなさい。**

犬の飼い主は、平和を乱したとして責められる可能性があります。それは、告発を決めてしまう程、犬が吠えることで隣人が困っているような場合です。

A dog owner can be charged with disturbing the peace (press charges / neighbors / its barking / if / so much / decide to / bothers / they / that)

____

(2) **次の日本語の意味になるように、ヒントを参考にしながら(　)を埋めなさい。**

鯨の腐りつつある体は不快であるだけでなく、破裂する可能性もあるので危険です。

Not (　　　　　　) (　　　　　　) the (　　　　　　) body of a whale (　　　　　　) (　　　　　　) it is (　　　　　　) dangerous because it may (　　　　　　).

ヒント：Not only is S A but it is also B「S が A であるだけでなく B だ」

(3) **次の日本語を英語にしなさい。ただし、(　)内の語(句)を順に使い、単語は必要に応じて変化させなさい。**

1 日に 6 缶のビールを飲むことは心臓にとって健康的であるとさえ言う人もいれば、一方で、1 日にそれだけ飲むことは肝臓の病気の一因になり得ると言う人もいます。

(drink; healthy; while; consume; contribute)

____

Chapter 15 Law! What Is It Good for?

観光地をハイヒールで歩いてはいけない（ギリシャ）

それぞれの文化の事情に応じて、変わった法律が存在するものです。この章では、法律そのものの意味と意義を掘り下げて考えたいと思います。

44

In Demark, there is a law which stipulates that drivers must turn on their headlights during the day as well as at night. A driver can be fined a maximum amount equal to about 100 US dollars if they violate this law. It is thought that lit headlights are effective in preventing traffic accidents. This shows that more emphasis is placed on safety than on conservation of energy. Therefore, one must be careful when renting and driving a car in Denmark.

In Canada, there is a law prohibiting shoppers from paying only with coins. Shop owners have the right to refuse to receive coins when customers attempt to pay over 10 dollars in coins. This law exists for the benefit of the shops, not the consumers. Many Japanese pay with coins to reduce the bulge of their purses, but it is better to avoid it in Canada.

In Greece, women should be careful in tourist spots. This is because they mustn't wear high heels that may damage any historical structures. So, the law protecting places of cultural and historical value in Greece encourages women not to wear high heels.

In this way, there are special and sometimes peculiar laws in the world, due to ideas or situations different from Japan. But from the opposite perspective, in Japan, there exist laws that seem strange to the eyes of foreigners.

In Japan, where human relations are considered very important, the ex-wife is prohibited from remarrying within 6 months of the divorce. This is done mainly to avoid any confusion as to which father the child born after the divorce belongs to.

Differing thought processes rooted in culture or tradition may cause different regulations or laws. Japanese may feel it is strange that eating beef is allowed in most countries but whale meat is not. This is based on the Old Testament's idea that only animals with split hooves and marine life with scales are allowed to be eaten. According to this idea, animals with undivided hooves like horses and marine life without scales, such as whales, should not be eaten. However, if whales were not an endangered species and could be farmed like cows, the act of hunting and consuming whales would be less of a problem.

Generally speaking, laws serve three purposes: to protect the natural environment including ecology, to protect human beings' rights, and to protect things produced by humans including cultural assets.

However, there are some aspects of laws that restrict people's civil liberties to an extreme level. This means that because of certain laws, some people cannot work or even live comfortably.

For example, artists or novelists cannot express their art or ideas freely due to censorship laws put in place to prevent slandering, embarrassing, or discriminating against specific people. There is always conflict between freedom of expression and the protection of the human dignity of certain groups of people.

It is true that since people who kill others out of anger could not be punished if it were not for laws, laws are a kind of necessary evil, but if the existence of laws is detrimental to a person's quality of life, this may be an example of putting the cart before the horse. Now is the time for us to think about what laws should accomplish and what laws shouldn't exist.

Words and Phrases

stipulate 規定する / **bulge** 膨らみ / **the opposite perspective** 逆の視点 / **remarry** 再婚する / **rooted in...** …に根付いた / **the Old Testament** 旧約聖書 / **hoof** 蹄［ひづめ］/ **scale** 鱗［うろこ］/ **endangered species** 絶滅危惧種 / **cultural asset** 文化財 / **censorship** 検閲 / **slander** 中傷する / **freedom of expression** 表現の自由 / **human dignity** 人間の尊厳 / **necessary evil** 必要悪 / **detrimental to...** …に有害である / **put the cart before the horse** 本末転倒

Tips

日本の計量法の不思議

日本には、計量法という法律があり、その第 8 条で、度量衡について国が認めた単位以外の計量単位を取引や証明の場で使用することを禁じています。

この法律によると、日本の伝統的計量法で、家屋の設計などには欠かせない「尺貫法」は、1958 年 12 月 31 日限り（土地と建物の計量については 1966 年 3 月 31 日限り）で、取引や証明での使用は禁止されました。違反者は 50 万円以下の罰金に処せられます。一方、英米の計量法であるヤード・ポンド法の使用は可能とされています。

1 VOCABULARY

次の日本語を読み、(　)に当てはまる語を選んで、英訳を完成させなさい。

(1) 日本人の買い物客は、カナダでは、財布のふくらみをなくすために小銭で支払うことを避けましょう。
Japanese (a. 　　　　　　) are advised not to use coins for the purpose of reducing the (b. 　　　　　　) of their purses when paying in Canada.

bulge　bulk　shoppers　store clerks　storekeepers　swell

(2) 日本では、離婚した女性は、離婚後6ヶ月以内に再婚できない。これは民法733条にある規定です。
In Japan, a divorced woman cannot (a. 　　　　　　) within 6 months of her divorce, which is (b. 　　　　　　) by Article 733 of the Civil Code.

bigamy　estimated　reconcile　remarry　speculated　stipulated

(3) 鯨は絶滅危惧種だからではなく、鱗がないので食すべきでないと言う宗教関係者もいます。
Some religious people say that since whales are without (a. 　　　　　　), they should not be eaten, instead of saying that they are an (b. 　　　　　　) species.

endangered　engendered　gills　scales　shells　unlimited

2 COMPREHENSION

A： 次の問いの答えとして最も適当なものを選びなさい。

(1) What is the purpose of the Danish law mentioned in the passage?
(A) protection of human rights　(B) traffic safety
(C) conservation of energy　(D) freedom of expression

(2) What should women NOT wear in places of cultural and historical value in Greece?
(A) split hooves　(B) long skirts　(C) a bulging purse　(D) high heels

B： 音声を聴きながら(　)内に単語を入れて問いを完成させ、英語で答えなさい。 45 46

(1) According to the (　　　　　　), (　　　　　　) is (　　　　　　) (　　　　　　) very important in Japan?

____

(2) According to the (　　　　　　) (　　　　　　), why aren't we (　　　　　　) to eat (　　　　　　)?

____

3 GRAMMAR

次の(　)に当てはまる最も適当な語(句)を(A)～(D)から選びなさい。

(1) In Japan, there (　　　　　) laws that seem strange to eyes of foreigners.

(A) is　(B) exist　(C) are existed　(D) have

(2) Due to certain laws, some people cannot work (　　　　　) even live comfortably.

(A) and　(B) but　(C) or　(D) nor

(3) If (　　　　　) were not for laws, we could not legally punish people who kill others.

(A) there　(B) we　(C) it　(D) that

文法のポイント

(1) there 構文の動詞：be 動詞だけとは限らない。存在・出現の動詞なら可能。
(2) 「A も B もない」の表現：not A or B と neither A nor B（=not either A or B）の 2 つが重要。
(3) 仮定法過去：if 節内は動詞の過去（be 動詞は were）、節外は助動詞の過去。

4 COMPOSITION

(1) **次の日本語の意味になるように(　)内の語(句)を並べ替えなさい。**

法律が人の生活に悪影響を及ぼしたら、それこそ本末転倒です。

If laws affect people's lives unfavorably, this is surely an example of (the horse / the cart / putting / before).

＿＿＿＿＿＿＿＿＿＿＿＿＿＿＿＿＿＿＿＿＿＿＿＿＿＿＿＿＿＿

(2) **次の日本語の意味になるように、ヒントを参考にしながら(　)を埋めなさい。**

芸術や文学の分野では、表現の自由と人間の尊厳の間に衝突がよく起こるものです。

(　　　　　) between (　　　　　) of speech and human (　　　　　) often (　　　　　) in the (　　　　　) of art and (　　　　　).

ヒント：freedom of...「…の自由」/ in the field of...「…の分野では」

(3) **次の日本語を英語にしなさい。ただし、(　)内の語(句)を順に使い、単語は必要に応じて変化させなさい。**

一般的に言って、法律は 3 つの目的を持っています。それは、生態系を含めた自然環境を守ること、人間の権利を守ること、そして文化財を含め、人間が作ったものを保全することの 3 つです。

(generally; serve; ecology; cultural assets)

＿＿＿＿＿＿＿＿＿＿＿＿＿＿＿＿＿＿＿＿＿＿＿＿＿＿＿＿＿＿

Funny Laws in the World		[B-784]
「世界おもしろ比較文化」 —法律から学ぶ文化事情—		
第 1 刷	2015年 3月 10日	
第12刷	2023年 8月 30日	
著　者	石井　隆之	Takayuki Ishii
	岩田　雅彦	Masahiko Iwata
	梶山　宗克	Munekatsu Kajiyama
	ジョー・シウンシ	Joe Ciunci
発行者	南雲　一範　Kazunori Nagumo	
発行所	株式会社　南雲堂 〒162-0801　東京都新宿区山吹町361 NAN'UN-DO Co., Ltd. 361 Yamabuki-cho, Shinjuku-ku, Tokyo 162-0801, Japan 振替口座 : 00160-0-46863 TEL:　03-3268-2311(営業部:学校関係) 03-3268-2384(営業部:書店関係) 03-3268-2387(編集部) FAX:　03-3269-2486	
編　集	丸小　雅臣	
組　版	木内　早苗	
装　丁	Nスタジオ	
検　印	省　略	
コード	ISBN978-4-523-17784-5　C0082	

Printed in Japan

E-mail　nanundo@post.email.ne.jp
URL　https://www.nanun-do.co.jp/

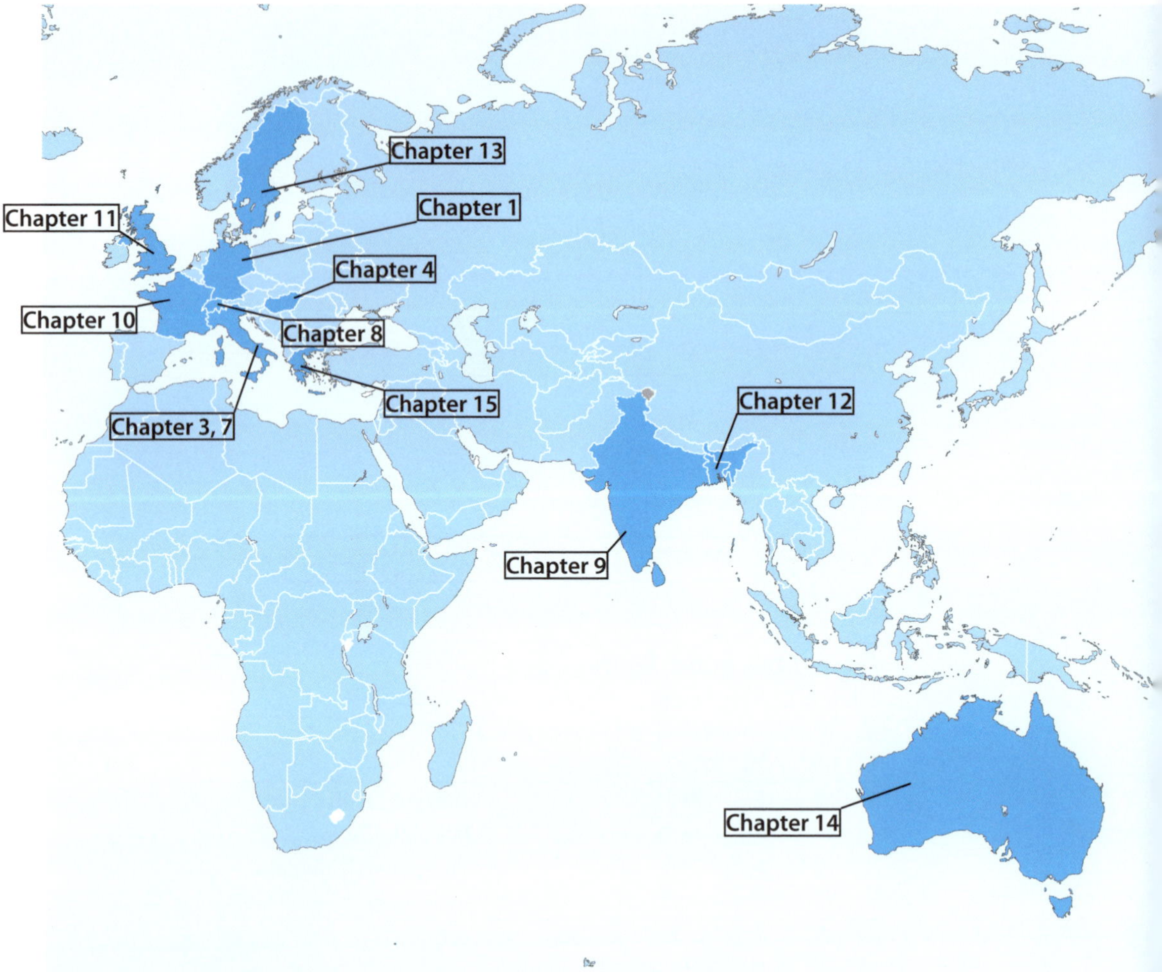

※ Chapter 6 に関しては、イスラム諸国を限定できない為、省略しています。

Chapter 1 What's So Free about Freeways?
速度無制限の高速道路，アウトバーン（ドイツ）

Chapter 2 Riding a Horse While Drunk Is Illegal?
飲酒乗馬の取り締まり（アメリカ）

Chapter 3 Walk Your Dog Three Times a Day!
犬は１日３回，散歩させなければならない（イタリア）

Chapter 4 Hungary Introduces a Tax on Chips
健康のためのポテトチップス税（ハンガリー）

Chapter 5 Don't Tie Alligators to Fire Hydrants!
「ワニを消火栓につなぐな」とはどういうこと？（アメリカ）

Chapter 6 Marriage and Divorce in Different Cultures
４回続けて同じ人と結婚できない？（イスラム）

Chapter 7 Smile!
葬式とお見舞いの時以外は微笑まなければならない！（イタリア）

Chapter 8 Silent Sunday?
午後 10 時以降，トイレは流してはいけない（スイス）

Chapter 2, 5

MEMO